✧ *Companions for the Journey* ✧

Praying with
Louise de Marillac

✧ *Companions for the Journey* ✧

Praying with Louise de Marillac

by
Audrey Gibson, DC
and
Kieran Kneaves, DC

Saint Mary's Press
Christian Brothers Publications
Winona, Minnesota

❖ *This book of meditations* ❖
is dedicated to the memory of Suzanne Guillemin,
Superioress General of the Daughters of Charity,
1962–1968, who brought Louise out of the shadows
and gifted us with renewed vigor
to serve Christ in the person of the poor.

The publishing team for this book included Carl Koch, development editor; Rosemary Wallner, copy editor; Rebecca Fairbank, production editor; Gary J. Boisvert, typesetter; Elaine Kohner, illustrator; Stephan Nagel, art director; pre-press, printing, and binding by the graphics division of Saint Mary's Press.

The scriptural material on pages 54, 59, 67, 80, 89, and 91 is freely adapted and is not to be understood or used as an official translation of the Bible.

The psalms in this book are from *Psalms Anew: In Inclusive Language,* compiled by Nancy Schreck and Maureen Leach (Winona, MN: Saint Mary's Press, 1986). Copyright © 1986 by Saint Mary's Press. All rights reserved.

All other scriptural quotations in this book are from the New Jerusalem Bible. Copyright © 1985 by Darton, Longman and Todd, London; and Doubleday, a division of Bantam, Doubleday, Dell Publishing Group, New York. Used with permission.

The acknowledgments continue on page 117.

Printed in the United States of America

Printing: 9 8 7 6 5 4 3 2 1

Year: 2003 02 01 00 1999 98 97 96 95

ISBN 0-88489-329-4

✧ Contents ✧

✧ Foreword ✧

Companions for the Journey

Just as food is required for human life, so are companions. Indeed, the word *companions* comes from two Latin words: *com*, meaning "with," and *panis*, meaning "bread." Companions nourish our heart, mind, soul, and body. They are also the people with whom we can celebrate the sharing of bread.

Perhaps the most touching stories in the Bible are about companionship: the Last Supper, the wedding feast at Cana, the sharing of the loaves and the fishes, and Jesus' breaking of bread with the disciples on the road to Emmaus. Each incident of companionship with Jesus revealed more about his mercy, love, wisdom, suffering, and hope. When Jesus went to pray in the Garden of Olives, he craved the companionship of the Apostles. They let him down. But God sent the Spirit to inflame the hearts of the Apostles, and they became faithful companions to Jesus and to each other.

Throughout history, other faithful companions have followed Jesus and the Apostles. These saints and mystics have also taken the journey from conversion, through suffering, to resurrection. Just as they were inspired by the holy people who went before them, so too may you take them as your companions as you walk on your spiritual journey.

The Companions for the Journey series is a response to the spiritual hunger of Christians. This series makes available the rich spiritual teachings of mystics and guides whose wisdom can help us on our pilgrimages. As you complete the last meditation in each volume, it is hoped that you will feel supported, challenged, and affirmed by a soul-companion on your spiritual journey.

The spiritual hunger that has emerged over the last twenty years is a great sign of renewal in Christian life. People fill retreat programs and workshops on topics in spirituality. The demand for spiritual directors exceeds the number available. Interest in the lives and writings of saints and mystics is increasing as people search for models of whole and holy Christian life.

Praying with Louise de Marillac

Praying with Louise de Marillac is more than just a book about Louise's spirituality. This book seeks to engage you in praying in the way that Louise did about issues and themes that were central to her experience. Each meditation can enlighten your understanding of her spirituality and lead you to reflect on your own experience.

The goal of *Praying with Louise de Marillac* is that you will discover Louise's rich spirituality and integrate her spirit and wisdom into your relationship with God, with your brothers and sisters, and with your own heart and mind.

Suggestions for Praying with Louise

Meet Louise de Marillac, a fascinating companion for your pilgrimage, by reading the introduction to this book. It provides a brief biography of Louise and an outline of the major themes of her spirituality.

Once you meet Louise, you will be ready to pray with her and to encounter God, your sisters and brothers, and yourself in new and wonderful ways. To help your prayer, here are some suggestions that have been part of the tradition of Christian spirituality:

Create a sacred space. Jesus said, "'When you pray, go to your private room, shut yourself in, and so pray to your [God] who is in that secret place, and your [God] who sees all that is done in secret will reward you'" (Matthew 6:6). Solitary prayer is best done in a place where you can have privacy and silence, both of which can be luxuries in the life of busy people. If privacy and silence are not possible, create a quiet, safe place within yourself, perhaps while riding to and from work, while sitting in line at the dentist's office, or while waiting for someone. Do the best you can, knowing that a loving God is present everywhere. Whether the meditations in this book are used for solitary prayer or with a group, try to create a prayerful mood with candles, meditative music, an open Bible, or a crucifix.

Open yourself to the power of prayer. Every human experience has a religious dimension. All of life is suffused with God's presence. So remind yourself that God is present as you begin your period of prayer. Do not worry about distractions. If something keeps intruding during your prayer, spend some time talking with God about it. Be flexible because God's Spirit blows where it will.

Prayer can open your mind and widen your vision. Be open to new ways of seeing God, people, and yourself. As you open yourself to the Spirit of God, different emotions are evoked, such as sadness from tender memories, or joy from a celebration recalled. Our emotions are messages from God that can tell us much about our spiritual quest. Also, prayer strengthens our will to act. Through prayer, God can touch our will and empower us to live according to what we know is true.

Finally, many of the meditations in this book will call you to employ your memories, your imagination, and the circumstances of your life as subjects for prayer. The great mystics and saints realized that they had to use all their resources to know God better. Indeed, God speaks to us continually and touches us constantly. We must learn to listen and feel with all the means that God has given us.

Come to prayer with an open mind, heart, and will.

Preview each meditation before beginning. After you have placed yourself in God's presence, spend a few moments previewing the readings and especially the reflection activities. Several reflection activities are given in each meditation because different styles of prayer appeal to different personalities or personal needs. **Note that each meditation has more reflection activities than can be done during one prayer period. Therefore, select only one or two reflection activities each time you use a meditation. Do not feel compelled to complete all the reflection activities.**

Read meditatively. Each meditation offers you a story about Louise and a reading from her writings. Take your time reading. If a particular phrase touches you, stay with it. Relish its feelings, meanings, and concerns.

Use the reflections. Following the readings is a short reflection in commentary form, which is meant to give perspective to the readings. Then you are offered several ways of meditating on the readings and the theme of the prayer. You may be familiar with the different methods of meditating, but in case you are not, they are described briefly here:

✦ *Repeated short prayer or mantra:* One means of focusing your prayer is to use a *mantra*, or "prayer word." The mantra may be a single word or a short phrase taken from the readings or from the Scriptures. For example, the short prayer for meditation 5 in this book is simply the name of Jesus. Repeated slowly in harmony with your breathing, the mantra helps you center your heart and mind on one action or attribute of God.

✦ *Lectio divina:* This type of meditation is "divine studying," a concentrated reflection on the word of God or the wisdom of a spiritual writer. Most often in *lectio divina,* you will be invited to read one of the passages several times and then concentrate on one or two sentences, pondering their meaning for you and their effect on you. *Lectio divina* commonly ends with formulation of a resolution.

✦ *Guided meditation:* In this type of meditation, our imagination helps us consider alternative actions and likely consequences. Our imagination helps us experience new ways of seeing God, our neighbors, ourselves, and nature. When Jesus told his followers parables and stories, he engaged their imagination. In this book, you will be invited to follow guided meditations.

One way of doing a guided meditation is to read the scene or story several times, until you know the outline and can recall it when you enter into reflection. Or before your prayer time, you may wish to record the meditation on a tape recorder. If so, remember to allow pauses for reflection between phrases and to speak with a slow, peaceful pace and tone. Then, during prayer, when you have finished the readings and the reflection commentary, you can turn on your recording of the meditation and be led through it. If you find your own voice too distracting, ask a friend to make the tape for you.

✦ *Examen of consciousness:* The reflections often will ask you to examine how God has been speaking to you in your past and present experience—in other words, the reflections will ask you to examine your awareness of God's presence in your life.

✦ *Journal writing:* Writing is a process of discovery. If you write for any length of time, stating honestly what is on your mind and in your heart, you will unearth much about who you are, how you stand with your God, what deep longings reside in your soul, and more. In some reflections, you will be asked to write a dialog with Jesus or someone else. If you have never used writing as a means of meditation, try it. Reserve a special notebook for your journal writing. If desired, you can go back to your entries at a future time for an examen of consciousness.

✦ *Action:* Occasionally, a reflection will suggest singing a favorite hymn, going out for a walk, or undertaking some other physical activity. Actions can be meaningful forms of prayer.

Using the Meditations for Group Prayer

If you wish to use the meditations for community prayer, these suggestions may help:

✦ Read the theme to the group. Call the community into the presence of God, using the short opening prayer. Invite one or two participants to read one or both readings. If you use both readings, observe the pause between them.

✦ The reflection commentary may be used as a reading, or it can be deleted, depending on the needs and interests of the group.

✦ Select one of the reflection activities for your group. Allow sufficient time for your group to reflect, to recite a centering prayer or mantra, to accomplish a studying prayer *(lectio divina)*, or to finish an examen of consciousness. Depending on the group and the amount of available time, you may want to invite the participants to share their reflections, responses, or petitions with the group.

✦ Reading the passage from the Scriptures may serve as a summary of the meditation.

✦ If a formulated prayer or a psalm is given as a closing, it may be recited by the entire group. Or you may ask participants to offer their own prayers for the closing.

Now you are ready to begin praying with Louise de Marillac, a faithful and caring companion on this stage of your spiritual journey. It is hoped that you will find her to be a true soul-companion.

CARL KOCH
Editor

✧ Introduction ✧

Louise de Marillac: A Legacy of Charity

Virtually unknown for 350 years, Louise de Marillac is finally emerging from the shadows of her mentor and friend, Vincent de Paul, and becoming justly recognized by the many thousands of women whose lives she has influenced. This recognition has led to an intense interest in her extraordinary life and spirituality among those whose hearts burn with charity for poor, alienated, or abandoned people.

Who was Louise? What animated her dynamic, revolutionary spirit? What forces urged her to respond with fresh insight and undaunted courage to the harsh demands of poor people? And finally, what wars did she wage within herself as she journeyed to God?

Louise de Marillac was a wife, mother, widow, teacher, nurse, social worker, and founder. She was an organizer, a radical thinker who lived her life intensely and enthusiastically, and a woman whose quest in life was to do the will of God with a deep faith in divine providence. She knew suffering, but she also knew love. Through this suffering and love, she became a mystic in action.

Why is it, then, that we know so little of this saint who was canonized by Pius XI in 1934 and declared Patroness of Social Workers by John XXIII in 1960? Joseph Dirvin, CM, who wrote the first fully documented biography of Louise, states that throughout the centuries it was assumed:

> that the dynamic Vincent de Paul had taken a weak woman and made her an automaton in carrying out, obediently,

humbly, and without a thought of her own, his charitable plans. Such an assumption does little honor to Vincent, who grasped the potentialities of this woman from their first meeting, or to God, who had prepared her for that meeting by an exquisite refinement in the furnace of suffering. (*Louise de Marillac*, p. ix)

Louise's Story

Louise was born on 12 August 1591, when her father, Louis de Marillac, was a thirty-five-year-old widower. The true identity of her mother remains unknown because baptismal records from the years 1590 to 1595 disappeared. Historians have suggested that her father married Marguerite Le Camus in 1590, but no accounts can be found of this woman or this marriage. Most likely, Louise was born out of wedlock and, by law, was illegitimate. Her mother was probably a servant in the de Marillac household and therefore, by social custom, not allowed to marry.

As an infant, Louise was placed in a Dominican convent-school at Poissy. This magnificent monastery some six miles from Paris was situated on the Seine River. Her father genuinely loved Louise and would visit her. He took great interest in her studies. During her twelve years there, Louise received a solid education in philosophy, theology, Latin, Greek, and literature. She was immersed in Dominican and mystical spirituality. Throughout her life, this formation in spirituality would profoundly influence her aspiration toward a direct union with God.

Precisely why Louise was removed from this convent school is unknown, but she left Poissy at about twelve years of age, around the time of her father's death. With her father's passing, Louise lost her home and the one person who truly loved her. She was placed in a boarding school near Paris. Life in the new school was completely different from the one she had led at Poissy. Here she received a practical education that included cooking, housekeeping, and sewing: all of the essentials appropriate to her state in life. Unbeknownst to her guardians and teachers, these studies also prepared her for her future as an educator and founder of the Company of the Daughters of Charity.

At this time in history, France was experiencing a religious renewal. This renewal awakened in Louise a desire to consecrate herself to God. At the age of twenty, she asked permission to enter the community of the Daughters of the Passion, but the superior of the Capuchins, whose permission she needed, felt that Louise's precarious health would not allow her to endure the austerity of the rule. His advice to her concluded with the prophetic words: "'God has other designs on you'" (*Vincentian Heritage*, vol. 12, no. 2, p. 123).

Marriage

During this era, families arranged marriages for their children. Michel de Marillac, Louise's uncle and guardian following her father's death, arranged for her to marry Antoine Le Gras, a secretary to the queen, Marie de Medici. The marriage took place on 5 February 1613, when Louise was twenty-two and Antoine, thirty-two. Although the marriage was arranged, true love grew between them. With Antoine, Louise found the joy and warmth of a family home, which was brightened by the birth of a son whom they named Michel Antoine.

Louise loved Michel, through whom, in his infancy, she came to know the profound joys of motherhood. But Michel, whose birth was premature, had difficulty developing, and he learned slowly. This seems to account for his subsequent drifting and often wayward behavior that would cause his mother many heartaches.

Seven years after their marriage, Antoine's health began to deteriorate, probably due to tuberculosis. He became despondent and angry. Louise loved and cared for her husband, but his mood changes and frequent bouts of impatience increasingly disturbed her. She took his anger personally and blamed herself for all of his distress. At a period when divine justice was a major spiritual theme, Louise turned to anxious introspection: Was all of this a punishment from God for her failure to keep her vow to enter the cloister? Was his pain all her fault?

Louise grew fearful and obsessed with her dejection and misery. Plunged into a torment of self-examination, she wrote in 1623:

On the following Feast of the Ascension, I was very disturbed because of the doubt I had as to whether I should leave my husband, as I greatly wanted to do, in order to make good my first vow and to have greater liberty to serve God and my neighbor. (Louise Sullivan, ed. and trans., *Spiritual Writings of Louise de Marillac: Correspondence and Thoughts*, p. 1)

However, during Mass on the Feast of Pentecost, in the Church of Saint-Nicolas-des-Champs, Louise received a *lumiere*, her light of Pentecost. She described the experience:

My mind was instantly freed of all doubt.

I was advised that I should remain with my husband and that a time would come when I would be in a position to make vows of poverty, chastity, and obedience and that I would be in a small community where others would do the same. I then understood that I would be in a place where I could help my neighbor but I did not understand how this would be possible since there was to be much coming and going.

I was also assured that I should remain at peace concerning my director; that God would give me one whom He seemed to show me. It was repugnant to me to accept him; nevertheless, I acquiesced. It seemed to me that I did not yet have to make this change.

My third doubt was removed by the inner assurance I felt that it was God who was teaching me these things and that, believing there is a God, I should not doubt the rest. (*Writings*, p. 1)

At home, her husband's illness continued, but Louise's fears about divine punishment had abated. For over two years, Louise remained constantly at Antoine's side until his last agony and death. With a heavy heart, Louise buried her husband on 21 December 1625.

Grief, loneliness, and feelings of abandonment nearly overwhelmed Louise. In addition, she worried about her twelve-year-old son and his future. Michel was a difficult child, but Louise realized that for almost four years he had lived with a sick father and a depressed mother. She felt responsible for much of his instability, and so surrounded him with excessive and overprotective love.

Louise wrote to her spiritual director, Bishop Camus, and explained the sadness in which she found herself and the trouble that invaded her soul. He responded:

> Mademoiselle, my dear sister, I do not know why your spirit is troubled and thinks itself to be in darkness and abandoned. For what reason? You are no longer divided. Now you belong wholly to the heavenly Spouse having nothing more to do with earthly things. For a long time now you have desired only Him, and now that He has broken your bonds and that you must offer a sacrifice of praise in the Host, you are astonished? Daughter of so little faith, why do you doubt? (*Vincentian Heritage*, vol. 12, no. 2, p. 130)

This harsh letter hardly proved consoling, but in many ways it foreshadowed the next changes in Louise's life.

Vincent de Paul

Because Bishop Camus lived far from Paris, he appointed a new spiritual director for Louise: Vincent de Paul. In the beginning, Vincent and Louise had scarce appreciation for each other. Vincent's simplicity was far removed from the refinement of Bishop Camus. Louise felt little or no affinity for him. For his part, Vincent only reluctantly accepted the spiritual direction of this young widow. He had just established a religious community of men, the Congregation of the Mission, for the evangelization of poor people. Also, his work with the Confraternities and Ladies of Charity and missions in the countryside placed great demands on him. But seeking to be obedient to what seemed the will of God, both Louise and Vincent accepted each other.

Later, both acknowledged that the providence of God had sent Vincent to Louise to be her guide and friend. Vincent, who was ten years older than Louise, had made the journey of faith, been tried by the fires of many trials, and his heart had been burned clean. Vincent listened to her suffering, and he understood. Their friendship would revolutionize the religious life of the Catholic church and its ministry to poor people.

As Vincent grew to know Louise, he discovered how much the rejections of her early life and the death of her husband had scarred her. He also discovered in her a great desire to know and to accomplish the will of God. Often he wrote to her, "Be then, quite humble, submissive, and full of confidence, and always waiting patiently the manifestations of his holy and adorable will" (*Vincentian Heritage*, vol. 12, no. 2, p. 131).

As Louise and Vincent became friends, Vincent taught her to trust God and herself.

Service to the Poor

In Louise's frequent contacts with Vincent, he described his work among poor people. He also told her about the Confraternities of Charity that he had begun in 1617 by organizing people in parishes to help alleviate the misery of needy parishioners. One principle guided the work of these charities: The poor are Jesus Christ. Vincent required that the personal service given was compassionate, gentle, respectful, devoted, and from the heart.

Vincent had also organized the Ladies of Charity, a coalition of wealthy women serving poor people. Most of the Ladies of Charity came from the nobility. They contributed generously of their time and money. However, because the French social custom frowned upon their doing menial tasks, their servants performed many of the direct services to needy folk. The servants often complained about adding these duties to their workload. Some took out their frustrations on the poor.

Louise gradually immersed herself in the work of the Confraternities. Indeed, throughout her life, guiding, organizing, and animating the Confraternities and Ladies of Charity would demand a majority of Louise's energies. Eventually, Vincent relied heavily on her judgment and organizational abilities, especially because the Confraternities were being rapidly established throughout France. Little by little, Louise gained confidence in herself. During these years, her mystic journey continued, and love for God burned quietly in her soul. Deep down, a healing process began to mend her shattered heart and restore her faith.

In 1629, Vincent received an appeal to visit the Confraternity of Charity in Montmerail. He wrote to Louise asking her if her heart was telling her to come also. Her heart did, indeed, tell her to go. So Vincent sent her "on mission":

> Go, therefore, Mademoiselle, go in the name of Our Lord. I pray that His Divine Goodness may accompany you, be your consolation along the way, your shade against the heat of the sun, your shelter in rain and cold, your soft bed in weariness, your strength in your toil, and, finally, that He may bring you back in perfect health and filled with good works. (*Vincentian Heritage*, vol. 12, no. 2, p. 148)

This journey began an intense collaboration between these two missionaries of charity, leading Louise to realize the creative potential previously locked within her. She grew to a new freedom, independence, and sensitivity.

As Vincent and Louise worked as a team, they discovered and appreciated their complementarity. Vincent and Louise combined daring initiative with prudent planning and constancy. Vincent provided the original vision of service to poor people, a vision shaped by the love of Jesus Christ. Louise helped transform the vision into reality. From 1629 on, Vincent guided Louise, and poor people taught her about a God who is more accepting, forgiving, and loving than the one she had known in her formative years. As God led Louise to the poor, charity burned in her heart so that she found and treasured Christ in the broken hearts, spirits, and bodies of the destitute people she served.

Founder

In 1630, while Vincent was preaching a mission, a woman named Marguerite Naseau came to him and asked to serve poor people. Marguerite was a peasant of about thirty-two years of age. She had taught herself how to read and had then gone about the countryside teaching young girls. At this time, peasant girls and the vast majority of peasant boys languished in illiteracy. Vincent sent Marguerite to Louise.

Louise, in turn, directed Marguerite to work with the Ladies of Charity in the parish of Saint Sauveur in Paris. Marguerite's example was contagious, and soon other young women came. They worked with the Ladies of Charity in other Parisian parishes.

Louise knew that these young women would need a strong formation, rooted in prayer, in order to persevere in their service. She also believed that it would be by faith alone that they would find God in the poor and the poor in God. In addition, she recognized that they would need mutual support and encouragement. As she watched the young women minister in the parishes, Louise became convinced that they needed a community that would dedicate itself to the service of poor, abandoned, orphaned, sick, and illiterate people.

Vincent decided to make a retreat to discern the will of God in regard to forming village women into a community. He asked Louise to pray for enlightenment. During this retreat, he became convinced that Louise's determination to form a community of service to needy people was, indeed, the will of God.

And so, on 29 November 1633, Louise welcomed into her home several young women who expressed their love of God and desire to serve God's *anawim*, or "little ones." The Company of the Daughters of Charity was born. Without consciously doing so, the Daughters dramatically changed religious life. Up to this point, religious communities of women had been confined to cloistered convents. Louise and Vincent had a radically new concept of how the Daughters of Charity should live their religious commitment. Not long before his death, Vincent spoke of the Daughters' way of life:

Having for convent the houses of the sick and that in which the superioress resides; for a cell a hired room; for a chapel their parish church; for a cloister the streets of the city; for enclosure, obedience, with an obligation to go nowhere but to the houses of the sick, or places that are necessary to serve them; for a grille, the fear of God; for veil, holy modesty; making use of no other form of profession to assure their vocation than the continual confidence they have in divine providence and the offering they make to God of all that they are and of their service in the person of the poor. (*Vincentian Heritage,* vol. 12, no. 2, p. 200)

The Daughters of Charity was a community of laywomen. In the early days of the community, they did not take vows. Later the Daughters began taking simple and private vows for one year at a time. The Daughters had to be free to go wherever the poor needed them. Given all of the restrictions of the time, becoming nuns would have prevented this freedom.

Years of New Foundations and Innovative Service

The number of Daughters who committed themselves to the service of what Louise called "the sick poor" in the parishes of Paris grew steadily. In 1633, five or six Daughters nursed the sick. By July 1634, there were twelve, and by January 1636, approximately twenty women had joined. The home of Louise soon became too small for the number of young women joining the community. So they moved into a larger house in the village of La Chapelle.

As the numbers of Confraternities, Ladies of Charity, and Daughters continued to grow, so did their works. Between 1633 and Louise's death in 1660, their ministry extended to foundlings, hospitals, galley slaves, children needing schooling, and elderly people. Three Daughters even began ministering in Poland. Louise maintained intimate involvement in these ministries by traveling to visit them, through reports from travelers, and through her extensive correspondence.

The Foundlings

In seventeenth-century Paris, an estimated three hundred to four hundred infants were abandoned each year in the streets or under the porches of churches. District superintendents brought them to an institution called La Couche to be fed and reared. However, the wet nurses and staff were too few. They gave drugs to the children to keep them from crying at night. The staff sold some to beggars who broke the infants' arms and legs, crippled them, so that they would extract the pity of passersby. The staff gave other infants to women who needed the status of being a mother.

In 1638, Louise organized the Ladies of Charity and the Daughters to take proper care of these orphans. At first, the women brought three abandoned babies into the community house at La Chapelle. Soon they rented another house so that they could care for a dozen more foundlings. Gradually, care of orphans and abandoned children became a central work of the Ladies and Daughters.

Louise embraced this work unreservedly and provided careful training for the sisters whom she appointed as adoptive mothers. Her writings provide exact directions about how the children were to be fed, clothed, led in prayers, educated, and so on. Many times Louise remarked that she wished all of the sisters could feel as God made her feel about the work with orphans.

Hospitals

Gradually, the Ladies of Charity and the sisters began ministering in hospitals. The Ladies of Charity told disturbing stories to Louise and Vincent about the treatment of the twelve hundred sick, poor people at the Hôtel-Dieu in Paris. Patients were forced to sleep several to a bed because of shortage of space. The epidemics that frequented Paris taxed the Hôtel-Dieu beyond its capacity. The hospital never had adequate supplies.

By 1634, the Ladies and Daughters of Charity began ministering in and reforming the Hôtel-Dieu. The Ladies were reminded to be cordial and patient with the poor people. Also, they should avoid wearing fancy dresses so that the poor people would not be unduly reminded of their poverty. Louise became so involved at the hospital that Vincent had to remind her to "take the air" to refresh herself after her "continual work at the Hôtel-Dieu" (Dirvin, *Louise*, p. 142).

Five years later, the Ladies and Daughters began administering the Hospital Saint Jean in Angers. So bad had the conditions become there that poor people avoided it unless they were dragged there bodily. Louise once again negotiated the agreement and directed how the hospital should be run. The

ministry in these first two hospitals established a tradition of hospital ministry that continues today.

The Daughters also gave nursing care in situations unheard of before them. During the civil strife that plagued France, Daughters of Charity nursed the victims of war in Rethel, Sedan, Stenay, Calais, and other ravaged towns and villages. They also nursed the wounded soldiers.

The Galley Slaves

In 1619, the king of France appointed Vincent de Paul to be chaplain of the galley slaves. Galleys—long, narrow, low-slung boats—were propelled by oar and sail. Even the most desperate men refused payment to row these boats, so the French government pressed convicts into service. The men wore heavy chains, suffered from hunger, fevers, vermin, and lack of adequate clothing. To make them work and to control them, their overseers whipped them mercilessly. Vincent did what he could to improve their lot, but he needed help.

In 1640, Vincent and Louise commiserated about the conditions of the galley slaves. Louise had visited them periodically since 1632. They decided that now was the time for the Daughters to minister to these outcasts.

Louise knew that the work would be dangerous and often repugnant. The men were bitter, angry, diseased, and crude. So Louise drew up careful guidelines for the sisters to follow in ministering to the galley slaves. The rules focused not so much on the safety of the sisters, but on the manner in which the sisters should treat the prisoners. For example, Louise told the sisters:

> The sisters must never reproach them nor speak rudely to them. Moreover, the galley slaves should be treated with great compassion, as much for their spiritual state as for their most pitiful corporal state. (*Writings*, p. 741)

She realized that the men would often resent even the good done to them. So Louise reminded the sisters that in spite of their vulgarities, filth, and crimes, the galley slaves were part of the Body of Christ who had become a slave.

Louise instructed the sisters to cook the convicts' food in their home and include meat and other nourishing ingredients. The sisters washed and mended the clothes of the galley slaves, and even replaced tattered rags that the slaves often arrived in. When the convicts left for work, the sisters aired and cleaned the cells. Louise performed these services herself when the occasion arose. One sister remarked that sometimes "poor discharged prisoners who were wearing rotted shirts on their back and whose legs were eaten away" would come to the sisters' house, and Louise "would wash their feet, treat their sores, and give them some of her son's clothing" (Margaret Flinton, *Louise de Marillac: Social Aspect of Her Work*, p. 112).

Practical woman that she was, Louise also admonished the sisters never to make matters worse by showing favoritism to any prisoner, by listening to pleas for help in escaping, or by ignoring any prison rules. She hoped that if the sisters acted prudently and patiently, the guards would learn to treat the convicts less harshly. In many instances, the sisters prevented worse brutality.

Petites Ecoles

In 1641, Louise inaugurated free schools for the poor little girls of Paris. These *petites ecoles*, or "little schools," tried to educate children wherever they could be found. The sisters also admitted wealthier children if they had no access to education. These children could come only on the condition "that the poor girls be given preference to the rich, and that the latter not look down on the poor" (Flinton, *Louise*, p. 96).

Louise sent the Daughters into homes and even farm fields to teach the children who were needed to help at home or work on the farm. If these children could come to school, but not on time, Louise instructed the sisters working in rural villages:

> Receive, at any time, any girl of any age who would like to come to learn. They must have the discretion to have those girls who are timid and bashful enter a special area, welcoming them warmly even when they come at mealtime or very late. (*Writings*, p. 743)

While Louise encouraged the school sisters to maintain regular hours for teaching, she added that exceptions had to be made

> in the case of poor little girls who go begging for their bread or those who are hired out to earn their living, which girls must always be preferred to others and must be welcomed whenever they present themselves and be attended to according to their needs. (Flinton, *Louise*, p. 98)

While Louise was sending sisters out to teach, she was also teaching the sisters, many of whom were illiterate. Louise taught them reading, basic knowledge of religion, simple arithmetic, and writing. Above all, Louise gave the sisters instruction on the duties of a good Christian woman.

The Elderly Poor

In 1652, Louise organized the Hospice of the Holy Name of Jesus. This was a home for poor, elderly people. Each person worked according to his or her strength and ability. The work mitigated the residents' loneliness, provided for their maintenance, and gave them a sense of dignity. Men wove and made shoes. Women made gloves and lingerie. Some skilled artisans volunteered their time to instruct the hospice residents in their craft. In some cases, the instructors received a salary.

Plague Victims in Poland

At the request of Marie-Louise, Queen of Poland, Sisters Marguerite Moreau, Madeleine Drugeon, and Francoise Donelle were sent to Poland to nurse victims of the plague that was ravishing the population.

Vincent de Paul related the news of this band of missionaries to the sisters in Paris. After the three sisters arrived in Poland, the queen gave them time to learn the language. Then the queen told them: "There are three of you. I intend to keep one with me, and it is you, Sister Marguerite. The others will go to Krakow to serve the poor." Shocked, Sister Marguerite blurted out, "Ah! Madame, what are you saying? There are only three of us to serve the poor; and you have in your kingdom plenty of other people more capable than we are to serve Your Majesty!" Taken aback, the queen replied, "What! Sister, do you not wish to serve me?" Marguerite answered, "Pardon me, Madame, but it is God who has called us to serve the poor" (Dirvin, *Louise*, p. 319). The queen backed off, and the three began serving Poland's poor. These were the first Daughters sent on mission outside of France; many more would follow.

Michel Le Gras

Even while Louise was assuming more direction of the Ladies and Daughters of Charity, she still tried to fulfill her duties as a mother to her son, Michel.

When he reached fourteen, Louise sent him to a junior seminary with the hopes that he would become a priest. Despite his limited abilities, Michel performed adequately for a time. During his twenties, Michel vacillated between pursuing the priesthood and leaving. Although his misadventures during this period are only vaguely referred to in Louise's writings, he seems to have caused Louise no end of headaches. Ultimately, he abandoned the seminary.

Then in December 1644, he disappeared entirely, leaving Louise anxious and upset. Some months later, Michel turned up. He had run off with a wine seller's daughter. Michel was brought to Saint Lazare, the motherhouse of the Congregation of the Mission, to be supervised by Vincent. The girl was sent to a monastery for wayward women.

For some years following, Michel continued to drift. Louise and Vincent used their influence to find him a position, but Michel took off again, this time with a male companion. After awhile, Michel returned. A friend of Louise, Madame de Romilly, introduced Michel to Mademoiselle Portier, hoping that the two would marry. Monsieur Portier, the young woman's father, rejected the arrangement, wanting a "good match" for his daughter.

Finally, Michel met Gabrielle Le Clerc, daughter of Lord de Chennevieres. The two families completed negotiations rapidly. On 18 January 1650, Michel and Gabrielle married. At the beginning of the following year, Louise-Renee was born.

Michel finally settled down. Louise-Renee provided intense joy to Louise. Her parents brought Louise-Renee to visit Louise so often that the sisters started calling her "the little sister."

Take Good Care of the Poor

Years of chronic illnesses and hard work finally brought Louise to the end of her time on earth. She died on 15 March 1660. To those gathered around her deathbed, Louise bequeathed to the sisters her great mission to serve the poor:

> My dear Sisters, I continue to ask God for His blessings for you and pray that He will grant you the grace to persevere in your vocation in order to serve Him in the manner He asks of you. Take good care of the poor. Above all, live together in great union and cordiality, loving one another in imitation of the union and life of Our Lord. Pray earnestly to the Blessed Virgin that she may be your only Mother. (This spiritual testament was recorded by the sisters who attended Saint Louise during her final illness). (*Vincentian Heritage*, vol. 12, no. 2, p. 254)

This simple bequest sums up the life of Louise de Marillac:
+ *Ministry:* "Take good care of the poor."
+ *Community:* "Above all, live together in great union and cordiality."
+ *Prayer:* "I continue to ask God for His blessings. . . . Pray earnestly to the Blessed Virgin that she may be your only Mother."

Love of Christ urged her to go to the poor, the sick, the oppressed, the downtrodden, the imprisoned, the uneducated, and the underprivileged. The poor did not lead Louise to God, Jesus led her to the poor. Her motto for the Daughters was, "The charity of Christ presses us." This is what Louise realized in her life, and this is her continuing legacy of charity to the ages, to the poor, and to us.

Today thousands of Confraternity members, Ladies of Charity, and Daughters of Charity all over the world continue the ministry handed down to them from Louise and Vincent. They serve in hospitals, clinics, home health care, schools, hospices, social-service agencies, homeless shelters, immigration services, and on battlefields: They serve wherever poor people need help.

Praying with Louise de Marillac

Louise possessed an intense love of God that was the foundation and the focus of her life. From 1627 on, Vincent's influence was reflected in her writings. Fundamentally, she came to realize that only by following Christ can true union of persons with their God be achieved. The following are some of the basic themes of her spirituality.

Being Led by the Spirit to Do God's Will

Given the loneliness and alienation of her early life and the illness of her husband, Louise found herself desperate to understand the meaning and direction of her life. On Pentecost Sunday in 1623, the Holy Spirit enlightened and inspired her. Henceforth Louise knew that she could rely on the guidance of the Holy Spirit when trying to discern God's will. Whenever a decision needed to be made or crisis confronted, Louise would pray for God's help and trust that it would come.

The Incarnation

Louise embraced the Incarnation as the most wonderful work of God in salvation history. Louise admired the humility of God-made-Flesh. Christ came "as humbly as can be imagined so that we might be more free to approach Him" (*Writings,* p. 700). She experienced the whole life of Jesus as a manifestation of the fullness of his love, and his pilgrimage on earth as a model for all of us to imitate.

The Charity of Christ Crucified

For Louise, to follow Jesus Christ meant our life needs to be a continuation of his. Imitating Christ calls us to change the world of poor and oppressed people and to actively serve those in need.

With so much suffering in her life and in the lives of those she served, she readily identified with the Passion of Jesus. She often signed her letters, "I am in the love of Jesus Crucified" (*Writings*, p. 278). Louise saw the poor in the suffering Christ. Love of Christ and love of poor people were inseparable in her spirituality.

Christian Hope

Christian hope resolved Louise's anxieties. She knew that hope was the only valid answer to people's sufferings. Hope is contagious, and her hope inspired her companions, collaborators, and the people that she served. Believing in the Resurrection, Louise lived joyfully. This joy and peace gave her the freedom to accept and to be accepted.

Louise for Today

Like Louise, we experience a fractured world, a world of suffering, deceit, pessimism, injustice, and futility. Louise knew personal pain and suffering, and she also knew the pain and suffering of God's poor people.

She welcomed the grace of God, which transformed her fretful heart into a courageous, generous, and compassionate heart that loved intensely; a heart that welcomed poor, hopeless, alienated, and abandoned people. She took a small group of young women and molded them into a community of total dedication, given to God in the service of the poor. She organized, directed, and animated the Confraternities and Ladies of Charity. Louise was able to do this because she loved and hoped in God.

Louise offers us the courage to face ourselves squarely, to overcome our insecurities and our inadequacies, to band together with Christ, and bring healing and hope to our broken world.

✧ Meditation 1 ✧

Brokenness

Theme: From the earliest stages of her life, Louise was touched by pain and sorrow. She understood rejection, grief, and alienation. Her pain drew Louise closer to God's embrace and to other women and men who suffered.

Opening prayer: Loving God, help me to understand that suffering can pave the way to deep joy and holy gratitude.

About Louise

From birth, Louise was marked as illegitimate. As an infant, she never felt the warmth of being cuddled in a mother's arms. At three years of age, due to her illegitimacy, she was sent away to a convent school, never to return to her father's house.

Her father married again when Louise was four years old. A half-sister, Innocent, was born when Louise was ten years old. The family never included Louise in its life, and she had to grapple with the fear that this new daughter would displace her completely in her father's attention.

Evidently, Louise's father did love her. He visited her at boarding school and took an interest in her progress. However, just before her thirteenth birthday, her father died, and she became the ward of an aloof guardian, her Uncle Michel. Her uncle sent her to live in a boarding house in surroundings totally foreign to her. In her entire early life, Louise never had a home and family.

When Louise was about twenty years old, she felt drawn to the religious life. In her loneliness, she sought the refuge of the cloister. She requested entrance to the Daughters of the Passion, a cloistered Capuchin community. They refused her request, citing her fragile health. Again, Louise suffered rejection. She felt that their refusal was really due to her illegitimate birth, and this was another intense blow.

Her director, Capuchin Father de Champigny, reinforced the decision of the Daughters of the Passion to refuse her admittance to the community. He told her that she had neither the health nor the vocation for the life of penance and austerity demanded by this religious community. But to console her, he added, "'God has other designs on you'" (*Vincentian Heritage*, vol. 12, no. 2, p. 123). Louise had no idea of the meaning these words held, but she pondered them in her heart.

Her marriage to Antoine Le Gras ended too soon. She had learned to love Antoine, but death took him. Even her child, Michel, whom she loved profoundly, caused her one grief after another.

Chronically poor health plagued Louise, but her major suffering came from inside, from her feelings of inadequacy, guilt, and insecurity. Being uprooted so frequently and feeling abandoned time and again undoubtedly shaped Louise's character. Ingrained insecurity haunted her for a long time, but it also compelled her to turn to and rely on God's love.

Pause: Reflect on your early life and identify those challenges or sufferings that have brought you to this moment but that you have only understood in hindsight.

Louise's Words

God, who has granted me so many graces, led me to understand that it was His holy will that I go to Him by way of the Cross. His goodness chose to mark me with it from my birth and He has hardly ever left me, at any age, without some occasion of suffering. (*Writings*, p. 711)

But souls chosen by God are very particularly destined to suffer, and this is such a sweet and agreeable privilege for them that they would rather die than not suffer since they consider loving and suffering as one and the same thing.

Our Lord wanted us to understand the dignity of suffering when he told Saint Paul that he would be honored by the privilege of suffering in His name. This belief is a truth which must be deeply rooted in our hearts. Effectively, what are we accomplishing on earth when we suffer? We are applying to ourselves the merit of the sufferings of Jesus Christ. (*Writings*, pp. 775–776)

Reflection

Louise knew suffering and rejection, yet she had a basic love for life. She did not allow painful circumstances to undermine her propensity to respond courageously to the challenges placed before her.

Linking love and suffering in the language Louise uses may seem quaint or slightly morbid. However, if we live long enough, we will suffer. Often love and suffering coexist. After all, suffering becomes magnified when someone we love dies, betrays us, becomes ill, or suffers any loss. To love means to be open to sharing the real lives of other people: their pain and joy, shadows and light.

God sent Jesus to teach us to love. Eternal life was reserved for those who fed the hungry, clothed the naked, gave drink to the thirsty, and visited prisoners (Matthew 25:31–46). Jesus defines compassion by all of his actions to relieve suffering. Jesus is "God-with-us" in all things, even suffering.

Jesus died on the cross not because God wanted him to, but because a person like Jesus who confronted injustice, who healed, and who loved so fully always makes enemies of people filled with hate. He died on the cross because the force of evil cannot tolerate such goodness. However, death did not have the last word. His Resurrection teaches us that those who die for love will rise to eternal life. This is the victory of the cross.

Louise came to understand and embrace Christ's cross as her own. To walk with Jesus meant that she walked the whole path with him. Her suffering, like that of Jesus, became occasions for and calls to love.

✧ Draw or write the story of your brokenness. Note each occasion of serious illness, abandonments, betrayals, and loss. Note how you responded to each suffering by answering these questions: Have I remained stuck in this suffering? Did this suffering transform me? Am I more or less loving because of this suffering? Dialog with Jesus about your story. Seek consolation and reconciliation about any unresolved issues.

✧ Meditatively read the "Louise's Words" section again. Spend time listening to Louise speak these words to you. When you come across a passage that is especially enlightening or perplexing, talk about the passage with Louise.

✧ This meditation may help you touch life's blessed memories and your experience of pain: points that have strengthened you and areas that may still need forgiveness and release.

First, relax. Get comfortable. Breathe slowly. If you need to, stretch your body. Close your eyes and enter into this journey. Imagine that your past is on film, and you are watching it.

Remember the people, the places, and the experiences of childhood, the sights and sounds and smells that comprised your life as a child . . . the warm affections . . . the fears and hurts. . . .

Allow these memories to flow into the present. . . . How have they shaped you? . . . How have they affected your relationships? . . . for good? . . . for bad? . . .

Which memories have sustained you in hard times? . . . Which memories still cause pain and need healing?

. . . Speak to the painful memories, and ask them why they stay with you. . . .

Now ask Jesus or Louise to sit with you. . . . Talk with him or her about the graces you need in order to reconcile with your past and about how your pain may be turned to love.

✧ Write a letter to God, asking about a certain situation that is not healed. Ponder your letter. Then, imagine what God would write back to you. Make an act of faith in God's love and mercy.

✧ Visit a pediatric ward in a hospital or volunteer your time with abused or abandoned children. Help to still their frightened hearts.

God's Word

Yes, I know what plans I have in mind for you, Yahweh declares, plans for peace, not for disaster, to give you a future and a hope. When you call to me and come and pray to me, I shall listen to you. When you search for me, you will find me; when you search wholeheartedly for me, I shall let you find me. (Jeremiah 29:11–14)

Closing prayer: Let us pray the prayer of Louise:

I adore You, O my God, and recognize that You are the author of my existence. Because of the love I owe You, I abandon myself to Your holy will in my life. Although I am filled with powerlessness and reasons for humiliations on account of my sins, I trust in Your mercy. I beg You, because of the love You have for Your creatures, to send the assistance of the Holy Spirit so as to produce the full effect of the plan which Your holy will has had, from all eternity, for my soul and for all souls redeemed by the blood of Jesus Christ. (*Writings*, p. 691)

✧ Meditation 2 ✧

The Light of the Spirit

Theme: The Holy Spirit, the living flame of love, will enlighten us during our times of darkness, if we ask.

Opening prayer: Come, Holy Spirit, enlighten my heart with your love. When life fills with shadows, light my way with your fire.

About Louise

In the midst of her husband's illness, Louise feared that their trials were divine punishment for her not becoming a nun. Thus, on 4 May 1623, she promised God that she would never remarry should her husband die. Even this promise, however, proved insufficient to calm her fears.

Louise also felt a need for a spiritual director more accessible than Bishop Camus. On the other hand, she feared changing spiritual advisers and did not know what to do.

Plunged into a torment of soul searching, Louise wrote:

On the following Feast of the Ascension, I was very disturbed because of the doubt I had as to whether I should leave my husband, as I greatly wanted to do, in order to make good my first vow and have greater liberty to serve God and my neighbor.

I also doubted my capacity to break the attachment I had for my director which might prevent me from accepting another, during his long absence, as I feared I might be obliged to do.

I also suffered greatly because of the doubt I experienced concerning the immortality of the soul. All these things caused me incredible anguish which lasted from Ascension until Pentecost. (*Writings*, p. 1)

Still despondent a month later, on Pentecost, Louise went to pray in her parish church, Saint Nicolas-des-Champs. During Mass, Louise received what she called her *lumiere*, her light of Pentecost:

While I was praying in the church, my mind was instantly freed of all doubt.

I was advised that I should remain with my husband and that a time would come when I would be in a position to make vows of poverty, chastity, and obedience and that I would be in a small community where others would do the same. I then understood that I would be in a place where I could help my neighbor but I did not understand how this would be possible since there was to be much coming and going.

I was also assured that I should remain at peace concerning my director; that God would give me one whom He seemed to show me. It was repugnant to me to accept him; nevertheless, I acquiesced. It seemed to me that I did not yet have to make this change.

My third doubt was removed by the inner assurance I felt that it was God who was teaching me these things and that, believing there is a God, I should not doubt the rest. (*Writings*, p. 1)

This light that she received from the Holy Spirit allayed many of Louise's fears, even if it did not resolve all of her difficulties. For two more years she continued to care for her husband in his illness.

Pause: Reflect on the words "the inner assurance I felt that it was God who was teaching me these things." Do you have such assurance?

Louise's Words

Do not be upset if things are not as you would want them to be for a long time to come. Do the little you can very peacefully and calmly so as to allow room for the guidance of God in your lives. Do not worry about the rest. (*Writings*, pp. 614–615)

Reflection

The Holy Spirit points the way when we are lost and groping for light. Louise found her way through the experience of light, that "inner assurance." The light of Pentecost had given her a peaceful respite and an indication of her future vocation.

She did what she could to aid her husband, guide her recalcitrant son, and manage her affairs. But she knew that the Spirit would be with her. This experience of the Holy Spirit strengthened her enough to realize God's presence in the midst of all her difficulties. Jesus gives us this same assurance. If we pray, the Spirit of wisdom and understanding will come to bring light to us too.

✧ Slowly pray this passage from the "Louise's Words" section: "Do the little you can very peacefully and calmly so as to allow room for the guidance of God in your lives. Do not worry about the rest." Let the meaning of her words become clear for you. What worries do you need rest from?

✧ One way of knowing that the Spirit and not our ego or compulsions is speaking to us is to apply this criteria: Does what I am hearing urge me to broaden the scope and depth of my love of other people?

Ask yourself these questions, and then meditate and write in your journal about them:

✦ Do I honor the Spirit who speaks through my intuition as much as I respect the voice of my reason?
✦ Have I ever felt myself prompted by the Spirit to take a course of action, but discarded the prompting because I could not believe it was from God?
✦ What have been some occasions when listening and following the Spirit have led me to greater love?

Pray to the Holy Spirit for wisdom concerning an important issue in your life right now. Be patient, the Spirit will answer in some manner.

✦ Much of our fear comes from our attempts to control the outcome. When Louise finally let herself trust the Holy Spirit, when she let go of the outcome and the answer that she had formulated for her problems of conscience, the Holy Spirit calmed her fears and gave her light.

Describe some situation in your life right now that has been vexing you, making you anxious or angry and afraid. Then ask yourself: Am I trying to control the outcome? Am I angry and fearful because I want to be in charge of what happens? How can I do what I can calmly, seek God's guidance, and let go of the rest? Dialog with the Holy Spirit about this.

✦ Many times the Holy Spirit speaks through our friends or even through the words of strangers. Who are your friends of the soul who can speak wisdom for you? How do you listen to them?

✦ In writing, describe the person you are. Describe the person you think God made you to be. What is the name God calls you? What is the Holy Spirit moving you toward?

✦ Visit an elderly person who lives alone, or visit someone who is dying. Listen and learn from this person. Pray with her or him.

God's Word

I shall not leave you orphans;
I shall come to you. . . .
The Paraclete, the Holy Spirit . . .
will teach you everything
and remind you of all I have said to you.
Peace I bequeath to you,
my own peace I give you. . . .
Do not let your hearts be troubled or afraid.

(John 14:18,26–27)

Closing prayer:

Yahweh, you search me and know me.
You know if I am standing or sitting.
You perceive my thoughts from far away.
Whether I walk or lie down, you are watching;
you are familiar with all my ways.
Before a word is even on my tongue, Yahweh,
you know it completely.
Close behind and close in front you hem me in,
shielding me with your hand.
Such knowledge is beyond my understanding,
too high beyond my reach.
Where could I go to escape your spirit?
Where could I flee from your presence?
If I climb to the heavens, you are there;
there, too, if I sink to Sheol.
If I flew to the point of sunrise—
or far across the sea—
your hand would still be guiding me,
your right hand holding me.
If I asked darkness to cover me
and light to become night around me,
that darkness would not be dark to you;
night would shine as the day.

(Psalm 139:1–12)

✧ Meditation 3 ✧

Waiting Patiently

Theme: Sometimes clarity about our role in God's plan requires us to wait patiently, trusting that God will lead us when we are ready.

Opening prayer: Patient God, allow my heart to be permeated by comforting joy and stouthearted confidence in your gracious goodness even as I wait.

About Louise

Sitting alone in her home after her husband's death, Louise had to reflect on her options. Her finances had contracted perilously. Physically she was exhausted, and nothing had prepared her for the utter loneliness that she felt.

Louise sent her son, Michel, to a boarding school where he could receive some positive male influence. Even though she felt that sending him away was in Michel's best interest, she sorely missed him.

In her despondency, Louise wondered what she was going to do and what God wanted her to do. As she waited, she began to recognize the need to rebuild her life in preparation for a clear call from God. So she composed a Rule of the Day for herself:

In the name of God and with His divine assistance, may I live thus!

> May . . . I . . . follow Jesus Christ and serve my
> neighbor with great humility and gentleness. . . .
>
> I shall meditate for an hour . . . on a subject taken
> either from the Gospels or the Epistles to which I shall
> add a reading from the life of the saint of the day so as to
> be instructed by a practical example. (*Writings*, p. 689)

In addition to these practices, Louise decided to recite parts of
the liturgy of the hours, then do her household chores, attend
Mass, work, do spiritual reading, eat, and meditate for fifteen
minutes. She continues:

> I shall try never to be idle. . . . I shall work cheerfully,
> until four o'clock, either for the Church or for the poor or
> for my household. . . .
>
> At four o'clock, even when I am in the city, provided
> I am not too involved in some charitable work or some es-
> sential social obligation, I shall go to the nearest church to
> recite Vespers. (*Writings*, pp. 689–690)

After Vespers, the rest of the day included meditation, supper,
examination of conscience, Matins, and the rosary.

Her Rule outlines other practices that she would follow
each week, month, or year. She ends the Rule with this prayer:

> I beg You, because of the love You have for Your crea-
> tures, to send the assistance of the Holy Spirit so as to
> produce the full effect of the plan which Your holy will
> has had, from all eternity, for my soul and for all souls re-
> deemed by the blood of Jesus Christ. (*Writings*, p. 691)

Louise believed that God had a plan for her, but that she had
to wait, pray, and do what she could until the plan took shape.

Pause: Recall a time when you had to wait for clarity before you could move forward positively in life. Ask yourself:
Did I wait with faith?

Louise's Words

The infinite goodness and wisdom of God leave the soul
free to draw on the infinite sources of His love. He is so

good that He communicates His prodigious love to all. This should keep my soul very humble and dependent on the divine goodness. (*Writings*, p. 701)

I must perseveringly await the coming of the Holy Spirit although I do not know when that will be. I must accept this uncertainty as well as my inability clearly to perceive at this time the path which God wishes me to follow in His service. I must abandon myself entirely to His Providence so as to be completely His. In order to prepare my soul for this, I must willingly renounce all things to follow Him. (*Writings*, p. 717)

Reflection

All growth to fullness demands time. The seed must be buried before it germinates and grows. The earth must be plowed and permitted to lay fallow or else it will wear out. In the fall of the year nature becomes barren. Winter waits for lush and fertile springtime.

We also must face the winters of our life. We lay fallow for a while. Often only then can we listen for the tiny, whispering sounds of life. Even so, waiting times can be frustrating, anxious, or boring.

Instead of waiting listlessly, Louise shaped her waiting with times for prayer, reflection, and service. She turned to God regularly, trusting that the Holy Spirit would shed light on the next challenge of her life. Indeed, through the charitable service that Louise gave during this fallow time, God called her to the great project of her life. But Louise had to watch and wait.

✧ When you have to wait for something or someone, how do you feel? What do you do? What do you usually think about? How could you use this time to talk with and listen to God's word?

✧ What are some questions that you have been waiting to have answered? Write them down. Then ponder how you can provide plowed ground for answers to take root and grow in. Do you pray and meditate over the questions? Do you seek perspective in the Scriptures? Instead of waiting listlessly, how do you wait with hope and trust?

✧ Meditate on the "Louise's Words" section. Read and reread the passage, letting its meaning for you become clear.

✧ Sometimes waiting for the Spirit to lead us means we have to follow Louise's advice: "to prepare my soul for this, I must willingly renounce all things to follow Him." Are there any attachments—such as pet theories, possessions, or self-concepts—that you need to let go of in order to hear God's word to you?

✧ Write a prayer of trust that your waiting will lead to the freshness of spring. Or, draw or paint a picture of your attitude of waiting and your hopes for the future.

✧ Poor people must always wait: for food in breadlines, for jobs, for medical help in clinics, for monthly government checks, for services. Next time you have to wait for what you feel is an inordinate amount of time, pray for poor people. Ask yourself what you could do—even in a small way—to alleviate the waiting for poor people in your area.

God's Word

We are well aware that the whole creation, until this time, has been groaning in labor pains. And not only that: we too, who have the first fruits of the Spirit, even we are groaning inside ourselves, waiting with eagerness for our bodies to be set free. In hope, we already have salvation; in hope, not visibly present, or we should not be hoping—nobody goes on hoping for something which he can already see. But having this hope for what we cannot yet see, we are able to wait for it with persevering confidence. (Romans 8:22–25)

Closing prayer: Gracious God, strengthen my resolve "to admire the working of Providence; to try to make known Its goodness and power; and to believe that it is a good thing to suffer and to await patiently the hour of God in very difficult circumstances, which is so contrary to my overly impulsive nature" (*Writings*, p. 495).

✧ Meditation 4 ✧

Discerning God's Will

Theme: Louise burned with the desire to do God's will, and her discerning heart searched for the meaning in the events of her life. She also came to know that God sends special people into our life to help us listen and stand in readiness to go where God leads.

Opening prayer: Merciful God, help me to listen for your will. May I patiently discern your will in the cries of poor people, the word of the Scriptures, the advice of wise friends, and in the yearnings of my heart.

About Louise

Seeking to accomplish God's will has always been central to Christian spirituality. Seventeenth-century French spirituality placed additional stress on doing the will of God. Thus, whether counseling a sister or asking Vincent for advice, Louise tried to keep God's will clearly in mind. To discern God's will, Louise recommended patience, prayer, and listening to the guidance of godly souls.

In her correspondence with L'Abbe de Vaux, an adviser to the sisters at the Hospital Saint Jean in Angers, we see Louise's trust that God's will can be known by patience. Writing about a young woman from Angers who expressed a desire to enter the community, Louise remarks:

I was immediately struck by her openness and good will, which disposed me very favorably to her request. . . . However, I have since heard that some of her relatives are trying to change her mind. . . . Nevertheless, she spoke in very different terms yesterday to Sister Elisabeth. If God wants to give her to us, He will certainly find a way. For my part, Monsieur, I assure you that I shall esteem and love her as if she were my close relative in the hope that we can work together for the glory of God. (*Writings*, p. 95)

God's will is done. We can only wait patiently sometimes for it to be done and for us to know about it.

This same patience for seeing God's will takes a humorous twist in a letter to Sister Marie Donion, serving the sick poor at Brienne. Because some sheets seemed to be lost, Sister Marie blamed her own negligence. And, evidently, a sheep appeared and then disappeared, upsetting Sister Marie again. Louise reassured her:

You may be certain that we often think of you and are distressed by the awareness that you are completely alone, although I have absolute confidence in the guidance of God and of your guardian angel. . . .

You must not worry about the sheets that were lost, since it was through no fault of yours. As for the sheep, if it belonged to you, you can say, "God has given it to me and God has taken it away. Blessed be His holy name in us and in what belongs to us!" (*Writings*, p. 627)

Indeed, God's will manifests itself often in the facts of the matter. For example, if a woman wanted to join the community but could not do the work, then apparently God did not will her to join.

Louise knew that even as we wait, we can pray to know God's will and that it be done when we know it. When the sisters were stretched too thin for the amount of work needing to be done, Louise wrote a sister in Angers instructing her to pray, but to be open to whatever God intended:

[God] will not fail us, my dear Sisters; let us be careful not to fail Him by not corresponding fully to His holy will. . . .

> Pray for the entire company and ask Our Lord to send laborers for His work if He wants it to continue. Requests [for more sisters] come from so many places that it is impossible to satisfy all of them. (*Writings*, p. 440)

Louise trusted her experience of God's guidance. The proof that they were doing God's will was that the community would grow. Meanwhile, they prayed for God to send more sisters.

Finally, Louise listened to advisers she had learned to trust as being filled with God's wisdom. Most important of all was Vincent de Paul. In their discussions about the affairs of the community, Louise would always present her thinking. Vincent would give his views. Louise saw divine will being discerned this way. In a letter to Sister Anne-Elisabeth at the hospital at Montreuil she says:

> We eagerly await the full report you promise us, begging God that it may be in total conformity with His most holy will. . . .
>
> Remember always, my dear Sisters, that it is the most holy will of God which put you where you are, and that it is for the accomplishment of His will that you must work there as would an ambassador for a King. . . . All must be done with gentleness of heart and humility, as we consider the interests of those with whom we are working rather than our own or even those of the Company. We were taught this by our Most Honored Father [Vincent] after he learned it from the Son of God, Jesus Crucified. (*Writings*, p. 208)

Louise honored Vincent's advice because it reflected Jesus' admonitions to love our neighbor and it led to good, and thus, had to be the will of God.

Pause: Do you pray frequently to know God's will?

Louise's Words

> Upon awakening, may my first thoughts be of God. May I make acts of adoration, thanksgiving and abandonment of my will to His most holy will. Reflecting on my lowliness

and powerlessness, I shall invoke the grace of the Holy Spirit in which I shall have great confidence for the accomplishment of His will in me, which shall be the sole desire of my heart. (*Writings*, p. 689)

I must have great trust in God and believe that His grace will be sufficient to enable me to fulfill His holy will, however difficult it may appear to be, provided the Holy Spirit is truly calling me. I shall know this by listening to the advice which He will permit me to receive. (*Writings*, p. 716)

Reflection

Although most of us would submit to the notion that we should follow the will of God, surrendering to it may be another matter. But knowing with surety what God wants in particular circumstances usually requires a combination of patience, prayer, reflection on our experience, and sound counsel.

Louise's practice of praying to surrender to God's will immediately upon rising recommends itself. We know that God wants us to love. The Scriptures and teaching of Christian tradition provide general guidance of supreme value. Ultimately, like Louise, we will need to ask ourselves: What does my experience suggest would be a Christ-like response in this situation? What is God—in the voice of others—inviting me to do? Louise learned to trust that the Holy Spirit would guide her.

She also sought sound advice from people she recognized as being in union with God. Once she became convinced that a certain course seemed to be God's will, she acted. Even then, she surrendered the results to God: if the work went well, God be praised; if it failed, they had misunderstood God's desires and should move on.

✧ Meditate on key events that have shaped your life. Ask yourself: How was God acting in these events? How conscious was I of wanting to do God's will?

✧ Reflect on some important decisions confronting you or situations that invite some response from you. Write down several, leaving room after each. Pick one to discern God's will.

✦ Pray to know God's will in regard to the issue; call upon the Holy Spirit. Listen to your heart.

✦ Reflect on your experience of similar matters. How did you act? What course of action proved most Christ-like?

✦ Go to the Scriptures. Read some passages that speak to your situation. If you have a concordance, use it to find passages on the theme. If you do not, open one of the Gospels, begin reading until you find passages that apply to your question. Ponder the advice you find there.

✦ Then go to a friend or mentor for counsel. Listen.

✦ Pray again for guidance.

✦ Decide if you can; wait if you must.

✦ Act.

✦ Offer God a prayer of trust, and let go of the results.

Use this process with each of the issues facing you.

✧ Who are people from whom you can expect counsel that is rooted in God's word? For those who have helped you discern God's will in the past, thank God and, if appropriate, thank them. If you do not have a spiritual director, consider seeking one.

✧ Talk with your spouse or a close friend about ways God may be calling you to serve needy people or to seek justice. Reflect together on this question: God's will is that we love our neighbor as we love ourselves; how are we surrendering to God's will in this regard?

God's Word

But you, Israel, my servant, Jacob whom I have chosen, descendant of Abraham my friend, whom I have taken to myself, from the remotest parts of the earth and summoned from countries far away, to whom I have said, "You are my servant, I have chosen you, I have not rejected you," do not be afraid, for I am with you; do not be alarmed, for I am your God. I give you strength, truly I help you, truly I hold you firm with my saving right hand. (Isaiah 41:8–10)

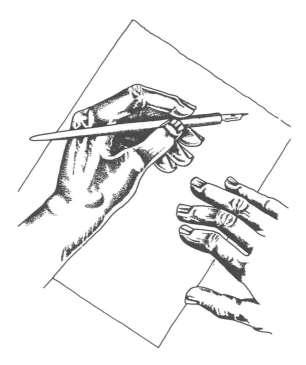

Closing prayer: Let us pray the prayer of Louise:

You desire to draw all to Yourself. Teach us truly to understand these words. If we belong to You, we can no longer belong to ourselves. If we believe that we are Yours, would it not be stealing to use ourselves and to live ever so slightly at variance with the precepts of the pure love which You taught us on earth? (*Writings*, p. 828)

✧ Meditation 5 ✧

Yearning for God in Christ

Theme: Louise hungered and thirsted for God, and through her prayer she absorbed the Scriptures until Jesus became her life. She sought to say with Saint Paul, "It is no longer I who live, but Christ who lives in me" (adapted from Galatians 2:20).

Opening prayer:

Like the deer that yearns
for running streams,
so my soul is yearning
for you, my God.
My soul is thirsting for God, the living God.

(Psalm 42:1–2)

About Louise

Before 1629, Louise's image of God was of a fairly distant, abstract, and demanding figure. Coming under the influence of Vincent and the poor people to whom she ministered, she gradually embraced the incarnate Christ as the human face of a loving God. Not only did she seek to do God's will, but she strove to put on Christ, to become one with God.

Christ was no longer a distant and awesome figure, but became an intimate companion to Louise. On 5 February 1630, while visiting the Confraternity of Charity in Saint-Cloud, Louise wrote: "At the moment of Holy Communion, it seemed to me that our Lord inspired me to receive Him as the Spouse of my soul and that this Communion was a manner of espousal. I felt myself more closely united to Him . . . and felt moved to leave everything to follow my Spouse" (*Writings*, p. 705).

In her retreat notes of 1632, Louise outlines the ways in which she tried to faithfully unite herself to Christ through imitating his life:

> Willingly must I allow Jesus to take possession of my soul and reign there. . . .
>
> Because Jesus took our misery upon Himself, it is only reasonable that we should follow and imitate His holy, human life. This thought absorbed my mind and moved me to resolve to follow Him wholeheartedly, without any reservation. Filled with consolation and happiness at the thought of being accepted by Him to live my entire life as His follower, I resolved that in everything, particularly in uncertain or questionable circumstances, I would consider what Jesus would have done. . . .
>
> All the actions and the entire life of the Son of God are only for our example and instruction. . . . This should give me great courage and confidence to undertake all that He will ask of me. . . . (*Writings*, p. 715)

One of the chief sources of finding out what Jesus wanted of her was the Scriptures, which she meditated upon for an hour each day.

Louise reflected especially on the Sermon on the Mount. In her manner of treating poor people, she strove to imitate Christ. This letter of 1648 to Sister Anne Hardemont, who was working with the sick at Montreuil, illustrates Louise's attitude about following Jesus by serving poor people:

> It is not enough to visit the poor and to provide for their needs; one's heart must be totally purged of all self-interest. . . . In order to do this, my dear Sisters, we must continually have before our eyes our model, the exemplary life of Jesus Christ. We are called to imitate his life, not only as Christians, but as persons chosen by God to serve Him in the person of His poor. Without that, my

dear Sisters, the Daughters of Charity are the most pitiful creatures in the world. (*Writings*, pp. 260–261)

For Louise, to serve poor people was serving Christ. Jesus was her model and her hope.

Pause: In what ways do you seek to imitate Christ?

Louise's Words

While reflecting on the divine gentleness during your periods of meditation, speak to Our Lord with great simplicity and innocent familiarity. Do not be concerned whether or not you experience any consolation; God wants only our hearts. He placed within our power only the capacity to make a simple act of the will. He considers this alone and the deeds resulting from it. Make as few reflections as possible and live in holy joy in the service of our Sovereign Lord and Master. (*Writings*, p. 679)

Blessed are those persons who, under the guidance of Divine Providence, are called upon to continue the ordinary practices of the life of the Son of God through the exercise of charity. (*Writings*, p. 821)

Reflection

Through the Eucharist, in reading the Scriptures, in charity to God's poor, or in simply turning her heart to God, Louise strove to unite herself with Christ. Indeed, the Christian journey is nothing else than the process of putting on Christ.

Desire to be one with Christ must be turned into actions. In the Eucharist, through faith, we partake of Christ's body and blood, in memory of him. The Scriptures teach and inspire us in the Way of Christ. Louise meditated on the Scriptures because she realized that an essential way of knowing Christ was to know his word. By feeding the hungry, clothing the naked, ministering to the sick—by being the love of Christ—we put on the love that Christ had. In surrendering our heart to Christ, we become like children, allowing ourselves to be embraced by our loving God. This is the Way of Christ, imitating him who was God and a human being.

✧ Meditate on these questions:
✦ How do I prepare for the Eucharist?
✦ What role does the Eucharist have in my relationship with Christ?

✧ Louise meditated upon the Scriptures, especially the Gospels and Epistles, for an hour each day in order to unite herself with the mind and heart of Christ. Ponder the role of Bible meditation in your life.

If you need a way of meditating on the Scriptures, a traditional approach is outlined here. You may want to meditate on God's word from this meditation, using this process.

1. Recall God's presence. Calm yourself.
2. Read the scriptural passage slowly.
3. Repeat as a prayer one word, phrase, or line that somehow seems most important for you. Let its meaning become clearer.
4. Read the passage again slowly.
5. Offer a prayer response, addressing God. You may want to focus your response on the word or phrase that you found most significant.
6. Again, slowly read the passage.
7. Ponder this question: How does this passage touch my life at this particular time?
8. End with the Lord's Prayer.

✧ Surrender your heart to Christ by spontaneously speaking with him. Tell him what is in your heart, realizing that he is listening. Then, slow down, be still, and listen.

✧ In order to remind yourself that Christ is the model for your life and your source of grace in all that you do, pray just the name of Jesus during the day. Start by praying the sacred name every hour and in spare moments; then try to pray the name as you walk, work, exercise, shower. Let the holy name become a melody always uniting you to Jesus.

✧ Write three adjectives that portray who you are for Jesus. Explain why you chose these adjectives.

✧ Louise tried to imitate Jesus in her service to other people. Ask yourself how you imitate Christ in the way you interact with your coworkers, your family, strangers, and enemies. Pray over ways you could more fully be the hands, heart, ears, and voice of Christ.

✧ Besides the services you ordinarily render to other people, go out of your way to do one gratuitous act of kindness to a stranger each day, remembering the adage:

Plant an act; reap a habit.
Plant a habit; reap a virtue.
Plant a virtue; reap a character.
Plant a character; reap a destiny.

God's Word

The bounty of God's grace, through the gift of the Holy Spirit, empowers you to grow strong in your interior life. Thus Christ may dwell in your heart through the faith that you have. So rooted and growing in love with all the People of God, you shall have the fortitude to take hold of the whole Way. Embraced by the love of Christ that is beyond comprehension, you may be filled with the infinite fullness of God.

All glory to God whose power works in us and can accomplish far more than we can ask or even imagine. Glory to God forever. (Adapted from Ephesians 3:16–21)

Closing prayer: Let us pray the prayer of Louise:

Most Holy Spirit, the Love of the Father and of the Son, come to purify and to embellish my soul so that it will be agreeable to my Savior and so that I may receive Him for His greater glory and my salvation. I long for You with all my heart, O Bread of Angels. Do not consider my unworthiness which keeps me away from You, but listen only to Your love that has so often invited me to approach You. Give Yourself entirely to me, my God. May Your precious body, Your holy soul, and Your glorious divinity, which I adore in this Holy sacrament, take complete possession of me.

Sweet Jesus! Gentle Jesus! My God and my All! Have mercy on all souls redeemed by Your precious blood. Inflame them with the arrow of Your love in order to make them grateful for the love that urged You to give Yourself to us in the Blessed Sacrament.

To this end, I offer You the glory that You enjoy within Yourself from all eternity, and all the graces that You granted the Blessed Virgin and the saints, together with the glory that they will eternally render You by this same love. (*Writings*, p. 834)

✧ Meditation 6 ✧

Missionary Zeal

Theme: Having discerned God's will for her and learned to trust God and herself, Louise now wholeheartedly gave herself to her mission of caring for orphans, sick people, galley slaves, ignorant children, and others in need. Zeal burned away attachments to anything that would distract her from her mission.

Opening prayer: Gracious God, fire of love, inflame my heart and empower my hands to zealously act with charity and justice and spread the Good News. May truth and goodness flourish in a world filled with shattered hopes and unfulfilled dreams.

About Louise

In 1629, Vincent asked Louise to accompany him to Montmerail to open a new Confraternity of Charity. She willingly went with him on this, her first, mission. For the rest of her life, Louise traveled extensively, setting up Confraternities, overseeing the works of the Ladies and Daughters of Charity, and ministering to poor people. She persisted despite chronic illnesses and terrible travel conditions.

Scattered throughout France, many of the Confraternities of Charity needed reorganization and revivification. Louise traveled on foot or horseback, by coach or boat. For instance, in

February 1630, she went to Saint-Cloud in the northwest; in May; Villepreux in the west; in October, Montmerail, east of Paris, and in December, in the north at Bouvais. At each place she tried to bolster people's energy, confidence, and enthusiasm. She also had to settle misunderstandings and make practical decisions.

Her zeal also urged her to expand the ministry of charity. In this letter to the rector of Notre Dame in Paris, Louise musters all of her arguments to convince him to open a free school in the parish; she is also not afraid to note her powerful supporters:

> Louise de Marillac, widow of Monsieur Le Gras, secretary to the Queen, Mother of the King, very humbly supplicates Monsieur des Roches, Rector of Notre-Dame de Paris, informing him that the sight of the great number of poor in the Saint-Denis district leads her to desire to take charge of their instruction. Should these poor little girls remain steeped in ignorance, it is to be feared that this same ignorance will be harmful to them and render them incapable of cooperating with the grace of God for their salvation. Should you agree, for the glory of God, Monsieur, to give the above-mentioned suppliant the permission required in such cases, thereby allowing the poor the liberty of sending their children free of charge to schools where they would be unhindered by the rich, who do not want those who teach their children to accept and keep poor children so freely, these souls, redeemed by the blood of the Son of God, would be obliged to pray for you, Monsieur, in time and in eternity. (*Writings*, p. 50)

Louise's zeal for the good of the poor little girls animates this letter. As children of God, they could not be lost.

Louise's missionary zeal also compelled her to see beyond conventional means of women ministering to poor people. When a self-taught peasant girl, Marguerite Naseau, showed up and offered to teach little girls to read, Louise immediately accepted. Soon other young women came to serve the poor. Louise brought these peasant girls into her home, taught them, and sent them out to minister. As months passed, Louise knew that it was time to form a community of women who would serve the outcasts of French society.

When she proposed this to Vincent, he discouraged her because at the time religious women had to live in enclosed cloisters. Louise waited and prayed for a clear sign. One day it occurred to her that her Daughters would not profess perpetual vows; thus, they would not be nuns. They would be laywomen, living in community, and take only simple, private, annual vows, including a specific vow to serve the poor. Equally revolutionary was that these were peasant women. Nuns usually came from wealthy families that supported the monasteries through dowries.

Her zeal had led her to break through hidebound concepts and create a whole new way of living religious community and serving the people of God.

Pause: Ponder this question: Have I ever felt zeal like Louise's to build the Reign of God?

Louise's Words

To Sister Genevieve Doinel at Chantilly, Louise wrote:

> I have truly been distressed to have left you all alone for so long and I praise God for having furnished me with the means to be able to send you our dear Sister Francoise. . . . I beg you to be an example for her of a true Daughter of Charity who is given to God for the service of the poor and who, therefore, must be more with the poor than with the rich; who has Rules to observe and no time to waste; who, except when she is required to visit the poor, must prefer her own house and the company of her sister whom she must love and support; who, consequently, must never complain to anyone about her companion or about anything that transpires between them, not even in confession where one must be careful not to reveal the faults of others; who must never speak of her neighbor . . . other than with great respect. . . . The Daughters of Charity are obliged, therefore, to strive to become more holy than religious. (*Writings*, p. 645)

Reflection

Louise had learned to trust in God and to trust in herself. Certain of God's love for her, she was free to live the remainder of her life in nurturing the poor. She now possessed an inner strength to face difficulties and to deal calmly with them.

A manifestation of the grace God showered on Louise was her zeal: ardent interest or fervor in pursuit of something. What Louise pursued fervently was the glory of God through service to the outcasts of society. Her zeal empowered her to cajole the powerful rector of Notre Dame in Paris; found a new type of religious community despite criticism, scorn, and opposition; and travel relentlessly to make sure that good was being done.

We may be afraid of the word *zeal*, but little of substance is ever done without it. When holy people have it, great good results. Christ calls all believers to be zealous for the Reign of God.

✧ Write a list or draw a poster that represents your bedrock beliefs or convictions that are your foundations in times of turmoil, fear, disruption, or doubt. Recall stories of times when these convictions and beliefs have fired your zeal for good or helped you hold fast to truth. Pray a litany of thanksgiving in which you thank God for giving you each of these beliefs and convictions that form the basis of your zeal.

✧ For what ideals or goals are you zealous? To answer this question, reflect on times in your life when you felt most alive, energized, when you exuded confidence that what you were about was good and meaningful, when you wished that you could hold the feelings for a lifetime.

Then, ask yourself:

✦ What happened to my zeal for these ideals?
✦ Who supports me in my zeal for these good things?
✦ Who cautions me to be lukewarm, to moderate my fervor for things that are important to me?
✦ Who do I listen to: those who encourage me to follow what God wants me to do or those who urge caution?
✦ What will happen if I continually dampen my zeal?

✧ Who are the people in your life for whom you have a strong, loving commitment? Meditate on ways in which you can nourish your zeal for each one's good.

✧ Louise exuded zeal for serving poor people. Christ calls all of his followers to this same mission. How can you zealously bring justice to your family, local community, workplace, and nation? Your ways may be humble, but also rich in passionate commitment.

God's Word

And as you go, proclaim that the kingdom of Heaven is close at hand. Cure the sick, raise the dead, cleanse those suffering from virulent skin-diseases, drive out devils. You received without charge, give without charge. Provide yourselves with no gold or silver, not even with coppers for your purses, with no haversack for the journey or spare tunic or footwear or a staff, for . . . laborer[s] deserve [their] keep. (Matthew 10:6–10)

Closing prayer: Come Holy Spirit, inflame me with holy zeal for goodness, for love, for building the reign of God. May I never be lukewarm in my response to your call to charity and justice. Grant me the grace to be "more holy than religious," more active in virtue than righteous in hollow words. Come Holy Spirit, inflame me with holy zeal.

✧ Meditation 7 ✧

Serving Christ in the Poor

Theme: God led Louise to encounter and serve Christ in the persons of poor people. For Louise, concrete, practical service to poor people could not be separated from serving God.

Opening prayer: Merciful God, open my heart to the needs of others, especially the poor. Fill me with your grace so that I always remember that in serving your poor I am responding to your love and fidelity. May my service take concrete form.

About Louise

Louise de Marillac shared her home, her life, and her daily work with the peasant girls who had the same desires as she did: to consecrate their lives to God and to the service of poor people. She knew that if these willing young women, the members of the Confraternities and the Ladies of Charity, were to persevere in their difficult ministry, they had to always remember that they served Christ in the people to whom they ministered. Louise embraced this ideal for herself too.

Once, a Lady of Charity wrote to Louise about some complaints that she had heard about the sisters at Bernay. Taking the complaints seriously, Louise wrote Sister Barbe to encourage her, but she added:

> Our vocation of servants of the poor calls us to practice the gentleness, humility, and forbearance that we owe to others. We must respect and honor everyone: the poor because they are the members of Jesus Christ and our masters; the rich so that they will provide us with the means to do good for the poor. (*Writings*, p. 468)

Louise repeats this advice many times in her correspondence with the sisters.

The belief in Christ's presence in poor people even touched a household custom of Louise's. On New Year's Day, Louise sent small holy cards with pictures of saints to the sisters throughout the missions. With the card, Louise sent this note to the sisters at Chantilly:

> We sent you your New Year's holy cards which are like all of ours. This is the saint who must show us our work since she was fortunate enough to serve the poor in the person of Our Lord, just as we serve Our Lord in the person of the poor. (*Writings*, p. 314)

This belief in serving Christ in the person of the poor had tangible consequences. Louise, the Ladies, Confraternities, and the Daughters assumed new works wherever the needs compelled them.

For example, in 1639, the Ladies and Daughters of Charity began administering the Hospital Saint Jean in Angers. This hospital, founded and equipped in 1153 by King Henry II Plantagenet in atonement for the murder of Thomas Becket, was in a dreadful state. Sick poor people avoided the hospital at all costs. Its governing body begged Vincent for help. Vincent turned to Louise. Soon the Ladies of Charity and the Daughters had straightened out the mess.

The desire to serve Christ in needy people caused Louise and the sisters to turn toward yet another neglected group: the young country girls who had no opportunity for schooling. The first sisters themselves often could not read or write. Louise taught them these skills so that they could instruct poor little girls. Eventually, Louise would send two sisters together to the villages, one to care for the sick and one to instruct little girls.

Louise outlined a regular schedule of prayer for her sisters, but even here she demonstrated the connection between service to God and to poor people. In a letter to Sister Laurence at Bernay, Louise reminded her that, "[Your superior] is well aware that we are leaving God for God if we leave one of our spiritual exercises for the service of the poor" (*Writings*, pp. 510–511). In prayer, the sisters encountered God, but also in nursing the sick poor.

Pause: Ask yourself: How conscious am I in remembering that Christ dwells in homeless people, single mothers on welfare, and members of street gangs?

Louise's Words

Oh, how true it is that souls who seek God will find Him everywhere but especially in the poor! How I cherish your thoughts on this subject! They gave me great cause to praise God. (*Writings*, p. 431)

Reflection

Jesus identified himself so intimately with the lot of poor people that at the Last Judgment we will be judged upon whether we fed the hungry, clothed the naked, and visited the sick and prisoners. Jesus ends by saying, "In so far as you did this to the least of my sisters and brothers, you did it to me" (adapted from Matthew 25:40). Louise took this passage completely to heart and then put it into action.

Christ does not want us only to see him when we see poor people, he wants us to take action. Louise saw a need and did what she could to alleviate it. And she never used as an excuse that the problems were so overwhelming that her efforts would be a waste. She did what she could, prayed for help, planned, and relied on God. On her deathbed, she reminded the sisters: "Take great pains to serve the poor" (Dirvin, *Louise*, p. 387).

✧ Reflect on these questions: Who are the poor around me? Who are the sick? Who are imprisoned? Who need clothes? Review the day's newspaper. Meditatively read the stories of poor people there. Then repeat as a prayer this phrase from the "About Louise" section: "We serve Our Lord in the person of the poor." If you are struggling financially, pray, "I am a member of the Body of Christ."

✧ In writing, ponder how poor people reveal God's life or presence to you. How has the example of Jesus helped to shape your attitudes about poor people? In what way does your attitude about the poor shape your life with Jesus?

✧ Fast or abstain one day this week. In your want, remember hungry people. Pray for them, and ponder how your way of life might contribute to unjust systems that perpetuate poverty. Set aside any money you saved on food purchases and contribute it to a local food shelf.

✧ Learn of and become involved in an organization that tries to eliminate the root causes of poverty and injustice. This might be a parish organization, the Ladies of Charity, the Society of Saint Vincent de Paul, Bread for the World, a Catholic Worker community, or some other organization. Consider becoming a member of one of these communities of charity.

✧ As a form of prayer, sort through your clothes, setting aside seldom-used or superfluous items. Clean and fold these garments. Pray for the poor people who can use them, and then donate them to an agency that serves poor people.

God's Word

Then [Jesus] said to his host, "When you give a lunch or a dinner, do not invite your friends or . . . your relations or rich neighbors, in case they invite you back and so repay you. No; when you have a party, invite the poor, the crippled, the lame, the blind; then you will be blessed, for they have no means to repay you and so you will be repaid when the upright rise again." (Luke 14:12–14)

Closing prayer: Let us pray the prayer of Louise:

[My God] may the desire for holy poverty always live in my heart in such a manner that, freed from all bonds, I may follow Jesus Christ and serve my neighbor with great humility and gentleness . . . honoring the poverty that Jesus Christ practiced so perfectly. (*Writings*, p. 689)

✧ Meditation 8 ✧

Our Manner of Serving the Poor

Theme: Louise taught that we are called to treat poor people exactly as we would treat Jesus: with competence, gentleness, compassion, and generosity. She understood that our manner of service is almost as important as the service itself.

Opening prayer: Compassionate God, through Jesus you taught us charity that was abundant, fearless, tender, and effective. May I learn from Jesus, so that my charity may be Christlike in action and in attitude.

About Louise

Louise expended enormous effort in correspondence with the sisters about the way in which they served the poor. She sent a summary of the Rule to the sisters at Richelieu. It contained the essence of their vocation:

> Gentleness, cordiality and forbearance must be the practices of the Daughters of Charity just as humility, simplicity and the love of the holy humanity of Jesus Christ, who is perfect charity, is their spirit. That, my dear Sisters, is a summary of what I think I should tell you about our Rules until such time as Divine Providence permits you to have the entire text. (*Writings*, p. 406)

The sisters were to treat poor people as they would Jesus. To reinforce this notion, Louise called the poor "masters." She told the sisters at Angers: "In my mind's eye I see myself now among you as you serve supper to our dear masters [the poor]. O my God! What a happiness you experience!" (*Writings*, p. 36)

When the sisters at Angers later began to lose their zeal for service, Louise upbraided them none too subtly:

> I can no longer hide the sorrow of my heart at hearing that much is to be desired in you. . . . Where is the spirit of fervor which animated you when you were first established in Angers? . . . Where are the gentleness and charity that you must preserve so carefully when dealing with our dear masters, the sick poor? (*Writings*, p. 113)

For Louise, kindness and compassion healed the spirit. This aspect of the sisters' ministry held an equal place with healing the body.

Besides kindness and joyfulness, service needed to be handled competently. Louise often included suggestions in her letters. In one letter, she asks Sister Martin: "Do you provide towels at the beds of the sick? Do you maintain their cleanliness?" (*Writings*, p. 182). To Monsieur L'Abbe de Vaux, Louise writes: "If you have not already been purged, I would be pleased to render you this little service by preparing you a potion . . . made up of . . . senna steeped overnight in a good mixture of refreshing, pleasant-tasting herbs" (*Writings*, pp. 46–47).

Louise also showed the Ladies and the sisters how to serve by direct example. On many occasions, the Ladies and sisters in various places asked her to send them more help. At one point, she wrote Sister Julienne Loret at Chars:

> I am likewise dismayed at not being able to send anyone to relieve you because, apart from the difficulty of the roads, we have never had so few sisters and been so pressed to send them to various areas. We just cannot furnish sisters because of the soup we are distributing everywhere. Here, nearly 2,000 bowls are served to the bashful poor. The same is being done in all parts of the city. (*Writings*, p. 401)

Civil war raged throughout the French countryside, and Paris was held under siege. Despite many dangers, Louise worked tirelessly with her sisters and the Ladies to protect and feed the refugees. True charity often requires courage; it almost always demands hard work.

Pause: Recall a recent act of charity that you performed. If Louise had observed it, what would she have said about the manner in which you performed it?

Louise's Words

I beg [the sisters] to renew themselves in the spirit of fervor, humility and cordial gentleness. . . . O my dear Sisters, it is not enough to be engaged in the service of the poor in a hospital, although this is a blessing which you will never be able to esteem enough. What is necessary is to have the true and solid virtues which you know are essential in order to carry out well the work in which you are so happy to be employed. (*Writings*, pp. 129–130)

Above all, be very gentle and courteous toward your poor. You know that they are our masters and that we must love them tenderly and respect them deeply. It is not enough for these maxims to be in our minds; we must bear witness to them by our gentle and charitable care. (*Writings*, pp. 320–321)

As for your conduct toward the sick, may you never take the attitude of merely getting the task done. You must show them affection; serving them from the heart; inquiring of them what they might need; speaking to them gently and compassionately. (*Writings*, p. 773)

Reflection

When a person seeks to serve, her or his Christian charity should be generous, gentle, cordial, persevering, and competent.

Charitable acts should be accompanied by a charitable attitude, so that both the body and the soul of a patient, student, foundling, refugee, or elderly person, indeed, anyone are served.

Louise treated poor people as "masters." This meant that she treated them as people worthy of complete respect and love. Christian charity not only acknowledges Christ's presence in the persons of poor people, but treats them as it would Christ himself.

✧ Reflect on these words of Louise: "What is necessary is to have the true and solid virtues." Examine your interactions with coworkers, family, friends, customers, patients, students, or other people you serve. Ask yourself: Are there any true and solid virtues that I need to develop to make my service more Christ-like?

✧ Talk with Jesus about this question: How do I reflect gentleness in my dealings with poor people, sick people, or people I find unattractive?

✧ Read the second passage in the "Louise's Words" section again. How do you feel when Louise calls the poor her masters? Do you feel the same way she does? Why or why not? Imagine that Louise is with you. Converse with her about your reactions to her words.

✧ Read and reflect on Matthew 8:28–32. Then compose your reflections to this question:
✦ What personal demons must I, with the grace of God, cast out of myself in order to be gentle, compassionate, and respectful toward people least likely to elicit these reactions from me?

Write a prayer beseeching God for the graces you need to be charitable in action and in attitude toward poor people.

✧ Pray for individual people, asking God's help in knowing how best to love each one. In addition, thank God for each one and the gifts that each gives to you.

✧ For her times, Louise acquired the competencies she needed to be an effective nurse, supervisor of a food line, servant to galley slaves, and so on. Knowing your skills and limitations, what knowledge and competencies could you acquire that would help you serve your sisters and brothers more effectively?

God's Word

Let us put on faith and love for a breastplate, and the hope of salvation for a helmet. . . . Give encouragement to each other, and keep strengthening one another, as you do already . . .

Encourage the apprehensive, support the weak and be patient with everyone. Make sure that people do not try to repay evil for evil; always aim at what is best for each other and for everyone. Always be joyful; pray constantly; and for all things give thanks; this is the will of God for you in Christ Jesus. (1 Thessalonians 5:8–18)

Closing prayer: Loving, compassionate God, may I always take good care of poor, weak, lonely, hopeless, ill-treated people—well, everyone—with gentleness, cordiality, forbearance, and competence. For this large task, I need your generous grace. Be with me, God, in both my charitable actions and in the manner in which I do them.

✧ Meditation 9 ✧

Relying on Providence

Theme: While on life's journey, we never fully understand the providence of God. We live our lives forward and understand them backward. Whether we acknowledge divine providence or not, God embraces us, sustains us, and provides for us at all times.

Opening prayer: Merciful God, I give you thanks for your bountiful gifts. You fill each day with blessings. In your providence, guide me in the ways of goodness.

About Louise

After fourteen years of existence, a serious crisis shook the Company of the Daughters of Charity and Louise de Marillac. The crisis did not come suddenly. At the end of 1645, warning signs appeared that the flame that had animated the first sisters was growing weaker. Some refused to leave the ministries in which they worked to go where the community called them. Others defied their Sister Servants (Superiors). Murmurings and criticism abounded: "Why must we always live in such poverty? Couldn't we look for a little more comfort?" In some places the sisters ceased treating the orphans and sick and needy people with the love and tenderness that Louise expected. Then in the winter of 1646–1647 many sisters fell ill and died. Others left the community.

All this turmoil caused Louise great suffering. Nevertheless, she weathered the storm. She understood well that suc-
cess has never been the goal of a life of charity. If God wanted
the community to thrive, God would provide. She expressed
this conviction to Sister Jeanne Lepintre in 1646:

> I praise God with all my heart for the guidance of His di-
> vine Providence. . . . It is Divine Providence alone
> which must keep us and provide for all our needs, partic-
> ularly those which human prudence can neither foresee
> nor meet. With all my heart, I hope that all our sisters will
> enter totally into these sentiments without ever relying on
> anything else. (*Writings*, p. 164)

> The next year, she reiterated her advice to Sister Jeanne:
> "Let us always adore the love and guidance of Divine
> Providence, the true and only security of the Daughters of
> Charity." (*Writings*, p. 226)

Pause: Recall a recent incident that caused you worry,
sleeplessness, or anxiety. Then ask yourself: Did any of my
worry help the situation?

Louise's Words

> Sometimes we are under pressure, and it seems to us that
> we urgently need and hope for help from others. How-
> ever, we are disappointed. This happens either through
> the conduct of Divine Providence or because of human
> weakness. We must then look immediately to the will of
> God and accept it in this situation. We should raise our
> minds to God and depend only on Him, remembering
> that, from all eternity, He has been and is sufficient to
> Himself; consequently, He can and should be sufficient
> for us. (*Writings*, p. 826)

Reflection

As time went on, Louise grew increasingly independent of her
friend and mentor, Vincent, but more dependent on God.

However, she feared that she was losing her friend, her support, her guide. This fear became a deep poverty for Louise, but led her to understand the deepest meaning of divine providence: God cares.

Knowing that God cares can leave us free to embrace our troubles and our deepest longings with incomprehensible trust. Fear comes in trying to control our destiny, the world, and all outcomes. Doing what we discern to be God's will and leaving the outcome to God's providence liberates us from much of our fear. Thus, we can gain a calm not felt when we try to rely only on ourself.

❖ We live our lives forward and understand them backward. We usually only appreciate God's providence in hindsight. Review the last several months. List some of the major ups and downs of this period. Then reflect on these questions: How was God's providence working in each of these situations? Did I seek to discern God's will in each case? Did each situation lead me to some good? If not, was it my fault, or do I believe it to be God's fault?

❖ Recall events in your life that reminded you that God is our "only security" as Louise says. If you need help identifying these reminders, most of them come in instances in which we experience fear or having no control. Converse with God about these times of dependence. Let God know your feelings.

❖ Part of God's providence is the family, friends, talents, and skills that God gives us. Praise God for the bountiful gifts you have been given.

❖ Sometimes we place our security in things: a job, a house, a relationship, and so on. Dialog with God about these questions: Are there ways in which I place more trust in possessions than I do in you, God? Have any of my possessions or relationships hindered me from following what I knew to be your divine will?

❖ Reread the "Louise's Words" section. Select one phrase or line that strikes you as important and pray it repeatedly, slowly, and calmly until its importance becomes clear to you.

God's Word

Stop worrying so much about what your next meal will
be, about how your body looks, or about dressing in fash-
ion. Human life is more than food. Your body is worth
more than the clothes draped on it. Watch the birds. Notice that they do not plant crops or store grain in silos, but
the Creator gives them food. You are worth more than
birds, aren't you? Can you add one second to your life
by fretting about it? No. And why are you obsessed
with clothing? The marvelous wildflowers do not sew
or weave, but not even Solomon with all his wealth was
arrayed as beautifully as a wildflower. So if God loves
flowers so much, even though they wither and die in one
season, don't you think the Creator loves you even more?

If you do not believe that the Creator will take care of
you, you do not have much faith. Stop worrying about

everything so much. God knows what you need. Rather, turn your heart and focus your attention on building the Reign of God in your midst. These necessities will be given to you as well. Do not worry about tomorrow; tomorrow will fend for itself. Each day has sufficient trouble of its own. (Adapted from Matthew 6:25–34)

Closing prayer: Let us pray the prayer of Louise:

I praise God with all my heart for such an excellent way of life, hard on nature but sweet and easy for souls enlightened by eternal truths and by the awareness of the joy to be found in pleasing God and in allowing Him full mastery over their wills! This, it seems to me, is the road that God wills you to travel to reach him, however difficult it may appear. Enter upon it, then, wholeheartedly as we would a vessel that will carry you wherever you must go. May Our Lord be with us as He was with His Apostles, granting them graces and preserving them. (*Writings*, p. 481)

✧ **Meditation 10** ✧

Simplicity

Theme: Louise sought to give her heart totally to God. Her spirituality became simpler and simpler: everything must be done for the love of God. Everything that distracted her from the love of God and service to God in the person of the poor must be discarded.

Opening prayer: Living God, grant me the courage to detach myself from anything that does not draw me to you. Fill me with your holy presence so that all my desires may only be for your glory and for love of my sisters and brothers. May I strip away distraction and simplify my life so that I can be filled with justice, fidelity, peace, and charity.

About Louise

Louise often called the sisters to simplicity of life. Rather than becoming involved in complicated rites and reflections, the sisters should, she said, "Speak to Our Lord with great simplicity and innocent familiarity. Do not be concerned whether or not you receive any consolation; God wants only our hearts" (*Writings*, p. 679).

Louise discouraged the sisters from trying to be sophisticated and from acting vainly. When some of the sisters began referring to her as "Reverend Mother" in their letters, she quickly responded, "Oh my dear Sisters, we are not the ones who should be using such terms! This is why I urge you to speak more simply" (*Writings*, p. 111). "Sister" was the only title for a Daughter of Charity. The director of a house was called "Sister Servant," and the dwellings of the sisters were "houses," not convents.

Louise urged the sisters to speak plainly to God and to one another, but she also knew that the sisters had to live and act simply for the sake of the poor people they served. Affectations would alienate the sisters from their "masters," who had at most meager resources. Louise remarked: "Remember, my dear Sisters, that it is the poor that you serve, that is their money that you are using, and that you must save every *sou* as a matter of conscience" (*Writings*, p. 222).

Because many of the sisters worked side by side with the Ladies of Charity, who were wealthy, they sometimes became tempted by the riches of these women. Louise recognized this problem and urged caution on the sisters. In a letter to Sister Barbe Angiboust, Louise gently but firmly reminded her of the need for simplicity, especially since she lived in a nice house:

> What shall I say to you about the beautiful house in which you live? Does not your profession of lowliness and poverty at times give you a twinge of fear? If so, I hope that you make heroic acts of virtue, both interiorly and exteriorly, so that you are ashamed to attract attention because you look upon yourself as the last and the least in that place, since you have only the food and clothing that God allows to be provided for you gratuitously. (*Writings*, p. 524)

If the sisters allowed themselves to be lured by the desire for wealth, they would lose their focus on serving Christ in the person of poor people.

Having received a superior education and come from a wealthy family, Louise had to learn simplicity herself. Suffering—chronic illness, the death of her husband, the stigma of her illegitimacy—had stripped her of attachment to what her world considered grand. Working with the sisters—uneducated, country women—and poor people reinforced Louise's simplification of her life. Her massive correspondence with the sisters shows a Louise who is focused, simple, and direct.

Louise always asked about the well-being of the sisters and sent simple admonitions, practical advice, and even hints about preparing low-cost remedies. Sometimes she chided the sisters directly:

> Remember to send us news of yourself from time to time. Do the same, Sister Andree, but, for the love of God, learn how to spell so that I can read your letters easily and answer you as you would wish. (*Writings*, p. 588)

> My God, sister Anne, what are you doing? If you are discouraged, I will tell you what I have already told you several times, namely that you must work. Laziness brings sin to the soul and illness to the body. (*Writings*, p. 587)

> If I am not mistaken you [Sister Laurence] are learning to write. However limited your ability to write may be, if you have a private matter to share with me, write the letter yourself. (*Writings*, p. 463)

Attachment to God and service to poor people demanded the full attention gained by simplicity of life. Simplicity had to be practiced by frugality, plain speech, modest dress, hard work, and an "innocent familiarity" with God.

Pause: Pray the word "simplicity" in harmony with your breathing.

Louise's Words

> We sometimes feel that we would like to perform great penances and extraordinary devotions, and we fail to realize that our enemy takes great pleasure in seeing us waste our time on vain desires while neglecting the occasions to practice ordinary virtues which are always occurring. Thus we lose the graces attached to these virtues by yearning for greater ones which God has no intention of granting us. (*Writings*, p. 481)

Reflection

Comfort, praise, and security can prevent single-minded witness to the Gospels. To live in union with God, people must be free from desire for and the shackles of wealth. Power over other people and abundant wealth are not the ends of human life: union with God is the goal.

Simplicity means that we live close enough to the limits of our resources so that we can rely on God's providence and appreciate the beauty of life. Simplicity fosters spontaneity, truthfulness, and clear speech. Simplicity also is required of anyone who seeks justice, peace, and equitable stewardship of resources.

Simplicity is not a simple way to live. It requires serious reflection to sort out what is necessary and what is luxury. With all the pressures to buy this and have that, it is difficult to be satisfied with having just enough, to be generous and caring. It is not simple to speak plainly and truthfully. We are tempted to equivocate, massage the truth, and manipulate our speech. Only conscious and consistent meditation, prayer, and examination can help us live the simplicity of Jesus.

✧ What possessions, desires, and unexamined notions clutter your life? Do a thorough inventory of the things that are superfluous and prevent you from being the simple, spontaneous, honest, and loving person that you want to be. Speak with Jesus about these matters; ask him to double-check your thoroughness.

✧ Considering everything you have, what is your most treasured possession? Does it own you or do you own it? Does it lead you closer to God and to love of neighbor, or does it make you cautious, overprotective, and suspicious?

✧ In a quiet place, alone, place before you a simple object like a spoon, bowl, or leaf—something of everyday use or commonness. Notice the beauty of the object. Write a description of the object or draw or paint it. Meditate on its simplicity and beauty. Thank God for simple beauty; pray in gratitude for the artisan who designed and made it, whether the artisan is human or divine; ask God for a simple heart to appreciate ordinary beauty.

✧ Sit quietly, breathe deeply. When you have calmed yourself, remind yourself again of God's healing presence. Then pray the following sentence over and over, letting its feelings and meaning permeate your consciousness: Jesus, meek and humble of heart, make my heart like yours.

After a period of praying this phrase, try to outline a "simplicity of life" plan. What would you give away? What would you keep? What are all the ways that you could enjoy life without spending money? To whom do you need to start speaking more plainly?

✧ Today, speak a few simple words of encouragement to someone whose life has become burdensome.

God's Word

"How blessed are the poor in spirit:
the kingdom of Heaven is theirs.
Blessed are the gentle:
they shall have the earth as inheritance.
Blessed are those who mourn:
they shall be comforted.
Blessed are those who hunger and thirst for uprightness:
they shall have their fill.
Blessed are the merciful:
they shall have mercy shown them.
Blessed are the pure in heart:
they shall see God.
Blessed are the peacemakers:
they shall be recognized as children of God.
Blessed are those who are persecuted in the cause of
    uprightness:
the kingdom of Heaven is theirs."

(Matthew 5:3–10)

Closing prayer: Faithful God, may I simplify my life so that my full attention is on what matters: loving you and my neighbors. Grant me the grace to free myself from all that may stifle my spirit and my service.

Mary, the Humble Servant

Theme: In faith, Louise confided her community into the hands of Mary. Louise asked her to keep the community faithful to its mission to poor people.

Opening prayer: Saving God, in choosing Mary to open the way to our salvation, you gave hope to all people. We ask that she be our companion and the companion of all the poor of the earth.

About Louise

In October 1644, Louise set out on the journey to Chartres. When she arrived, she went to the cathedral to pray to Our Lady. On Monday, 17 October, she confided the burgeoning company to Mary.

> We arrived in Chartres on Friday, October 14. My devotion for Saturday was to render to God, in the Chapel of the Blessed Virgin, the thanks I owe Him for the many graces that I have received from His goodness.
>
> Sunday's devotions were for the needs of my son. On Monday, Feast of the Dedication of the Church of Chartres, I offered to God the designs of His Providence on the Company of the Daughters of Charity. I offered the said Company entirely to Him, asking Him to destroy it

rather than let it be established contrary to His holy will. I asked for it, through the prayers of the Holy Virgin, Mother and Guardian of the said Company, the purity of which it stands in need. Looking upon the Blessed Virgin as the fulfillment of the promises of God to mankind, and seeing the fulfillment of the vow of the Blessed Virgin in the accomplishment of the mystery of the Incarnation, I asked Him for the grace of fidelity for the Company through the merits of the Blood of the Son of God and of Mary. I prayed also that He might be the strong and loving bond that unites the hearts of all the sisters in imitation of the union of the three Divine Persons.

In my prayers for myself, I placed in the hands of the Blessed Virgin the decision to be made concerning the outlines which I have given to my Most Honored Spiritual Father, as well as my desire for practices to help me to prepare for death while awaiting the plan of God in my daily life through the practice of holy obedience. (*Writings*, pp. 121–122)

For Louise, Mary was the exemplar for adhering to God's will, despite difficulties throughout her life. Louise likewise desired to follow faithfully the will of God, especially in serving the needy people who came to the Company.

Pause: Ask yourself: What virtues of Mary do I especially need to ask God's grace to acquire?

Louise's Words

I gaze upon you today, most pure Virgin Mother of Grace, since it was you who not only provided the matter for the formation of the sacred body of your Son, at a time when you were not as yet actually a mother, but by bringing him into the world, you have become both Mother of God and Mother of the Man who at His birth brought a new law to the world, the law which alone leads to eternal life. You are the Mother of the Law of Grace because you are the Mother of Grace incarnate. It seems to me that I have never looked upon you as such. If the people of Israel held Moses in such high esteem because they had received the revelation of the will of God through him, what love and service must I not render to you for having brought the God of the Law of Grace into this world. I shall manifest my gratitude to you by the praise I offer, by my zeal in helping others to recognize your greatness, and by renewed devotion and trust in your powerful intercession with God. (*Writings*, p. 775)

Reflection

Under Jewish religious law, Mary's unconditional yes to God's invitation could have resulted in her being stoned to death. Only her complete trust in God's will allowed her fears and doubts to be transformed to an act of courageous acceptance.

In her prayer of thanksgiving, Mary acknowledges that by selecting her, a humble, unknown young woman, God was manifesting solidarity with hungry and powerless women and men: "You have . . . raised the lowly to high places. The hungry you have given every good thing" (adapted from Luke 1:52–53). Indeed, Mary knew suffering and oppression. She serves as a model of the mercy of God toward poor people.

For Louise and the entire Company, to accomplish the design of God meant living as humble servants given to God for the liberation and salvation of poor, oppressed, ignorant, or sick people. In establishing Mary as mother of the Company, Louise asked her to guide each sister toward the full acceptance of the vocation given to them. Mary would help the sisters recognize Christ in all those they met.

✧ Mary accepted God's invitation not from pressure, but out of love. She chose freely. As a woman of her time, she understood the precariousness of her choice. Meditate on your choices:

✦ Are you facing any decisions right now with which you especially need God's guidance?
✦ Ask this question about each choice: If I were to discuss this choice with Mary, what would she advise?
✦ Pray for God's Spirit to direct you toward life, love, and hope in your decision.

✧ God chose Mary, an unknown, humble, young, unmarried woman to be the mother of the Messiah, showing once again that God selects the people of good heart to bear the Good News. Pray for a good and open heart and for a clear insight into how you are to bear the Good News.

✧ Louise realized that one way we give praise is by our "zeal in helping others to recognize your greatness." Examine your normal day. Identify ways in which you help others recognize God's goodness by your charitable deeds, listening, attentiveness, and way of speaking. Ask God to help you spread the Good News in your ordinary, day-to-day living.

✧ With her heart bursting, Mary journeyed to her aging cousin Elizabeth and proclaimed her Magnificat that Christ's power will reverse the order of things for the poor and lowly people. Make your own journey to someone in need. Be the Good News for them by your kindness, sensitivity, and aid. Listen well. Allow this person's journey of faith to be a source of strength to you.

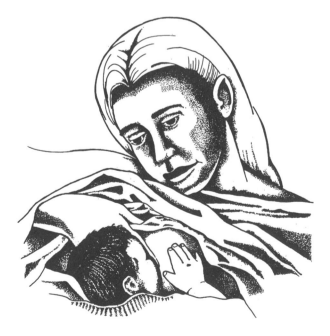

God's Word

My being proclaims your greatness,
and my spirit finds joy in you, God my Savior.
For you have looked upon me, your servant, in my
    lowliness;
all ages to come shall call me blessed.
God, you who are mighty, have done great things for me.
Holy is your name.
Your mercy is from age to age toward those who fear you.
You have shown might with your arm
and confused the proud in their inmost thoughts.
You have deposed the mighty from their thrones
and raised the lowly to high places.
The hungry you have given every good thing
while the rich you have sent away empty.
You have upheld Israel your servant, ever mindful of
your mercy—
even as you promised our ancestors;
promised Abraham, Sarah, and their descendants forever.

(Adapted from Luke 1:46–55)

Closing prayer: Let us pray the prayer of Louise:

I am entirely yours, most Holy Virgin, that I may more perfectly belong to God. Teach me, therefore, to imitate your holy life by fulfilling the designs of God in my life. I very humbly beg you to assist me. You know my weakness. You see the desires of my heart. Supply for my powerlessness and negligence by your prayers. (*Writings*, p. 695)

✧　Meditation 12　✧

The Strengthening Power of Prayer

Theme: Faced with the constant demands of serving needy people, leading a new community, maintaining her correspondence, traveling, and dealing with her son and his problems, Louise constantly turned to prayer for light and strength. God's grace flowed to her through prayer, empowering and illuminating her way.

Opening prayer: God of healing, God of strength, draw me to pray fervently, simply, openly, and wholeheartedly. May I trust in you enough to know that my prayer will be heard, cherished, and responded to with love no matter how inadequate my words or mixed my motives.

About Louise

While on retreat in 1632, Louise recommitted herself to prayer, writing in her journal: "I must have great trust in God and believe that His grace will be sufficient to enable me to fulfill His holy will, however difficult it may appear to be" (*Writings*, p. 716). In the years to follow as the Confraternities, groups of Ladies, and the community grew with all the attendant challenges, Louise prayed for and relied more and more heavily on God's strength as her own waned.

Louise composed her life in a balance between prayer and ministry, and she urged the sisters to do likewise. In her instructions to the sisters sent to Montreuil to begin a new work, she told them:

> Great gentleness and cordiality are necessary in order to win over these people. This is why it would be well if every morning each sister would individually pray . . . for the blessing of our good God in order that they might act in the manner of His Son while He was on earth as they carry out the works of charity to which they have been called. Better yet, they should pray that the same Spirit that acted in Him should act through them. (*Writings*, p. 773)

Louise knew that if prayer became an important part of the sisters' ordinary life, it would strengthen them during extraordinary trials, like the civil strife that broke out in France.

From 1648 to 1653, civil war tore France apart. The taxes to maintain the country's armed forces in its war with Spain and Austria became so burdensome that the people rose in revolt. Called the Fronde, the revolutionaries included members of Parliament, nobles, peasants, and merchants, all in opposition to the prime minister, Cardinal Mazarin. The revolutionaries barricaded Paris.

Hearing of the situation while visiting Liancourt, Louise hurriedly sent a letter to Julienne Loret, the directress of the seminary (novitiate):

> I am very troubled by a rumor which went around the countryside that there was unrest and murder in the streets of Paris. In the name of God, my dear Sister, send me news as soon as you can about Monsieur Vincent, my son and our sisters. (*Writings*, p. 257)

Louise worried especially about the sisters and foundlings since the shelter had been invaded.

As ever in these situations, Louise prayed:

> Let us give God the glory which we owe Him in the state in which He has placed us. I beg Him with all my heart to let you know how good it is to trust Him. . . . I beg the

Blessed Virgin to be your protectress and to obtain for you from her Son the generosity you need. (*Writings*, p. 277)

In March 1649, Mazarin and Parliament signed a peace treaty. Louise wrote to Vincent who had been away from Paris: "I will let others tell you the news of peace. I only know that it inspires us to praise God with the people" (*Writings*, p. 279). In sorrow and rejoicing, Louise praised God.

The peace was short-lived. In 1650, fighting raged in the Ardennes region of France. After the battle at Rethel, fifteen hundred dead soldiers remained unburied. Vincent sent some missionaries to lay them to rest. Two Daughters of Charity went to care for the sick and wounded, and the starving and homeless people. Louise encouraged them to abandon themselves to God's care in prayer:

> All our sisters ask to be remembered to you, and they praise God for the courage His goodness gives you to serve these poor afflicted people. Oh, what a grace, my dear Sister, to have been chosen for this holy employment! It is true that it is extremely difficult, but it is because of this that the grace of God acting in you is more evident. You have every reason to trust in God and to abandon yourself to His Divine Providence. God will never fail to let you know how agreeable this manner of acting is to Him. (*Writings*, p. 354)

Pause: Ponder this question: Do I pray only in the difficult times?

Louise's Words

It seems to me that our interior conversation with God should consist in the continuous remembrance of His holy presence. We must adore Him every hour and make acts of love for His goodness. . . .

We should raise our minds to God and depend only on Him, remembering that, from all eternity, He has been and is sufficient to Himself; consequently, He can and should be sufficient for us. . . . We must strive to keep our minds closely united to God. Such acts must stem from our wills. Therefore, I think that it is an excellent means of keeping our minds directed toward God as is His good pleasure.

. . . We must develop the practice of making frequent acts of the desire to know God and ourselves. This will lead us to make the repeated acts of love which we owe Him and to avoid anything that is displeasing to Him. We must often abandon ourselves to Him; show Him our hearts filled with trust and gratitude; and try, from time to time, to whisper . . . prayers to Him. (*Writings*, pp. 825–826)

It is your prayers . . . which attract from the goodness of God all His graces. (*Writings*, p. 160)

Reflection

Prayer was the source of peace, strength, and understanding during ordinary times and periods of danger and distress. Although Louise was physically weak much of the time, prayer gave her energy when she needed it. When the Ladies or sisters inspired or disappointed her, Louise prayed for them. And always, she prayed for poor people and those who ministered to them.

In her letters, the Rule, and other writings, Louise makes clear that prayer can be done in many different forms: meditation, a simple recalling of God's presence, sentence-long, whispered prayers, petitions, examinations of conscience, songs of thanksgiving, or simply opening our heart to God.

Louise urged the sisters to pray regularly. They needed to acquire the habit of prayer during the ordinary times, so that when grave challenges faced them, prayer would be their ready strength; they would turn to it readily, easily, and confidently. This remains wise advice for all Christians.

✧ Meditatively read the "Louise's Words" section again. Find one line that speaks to you in some special way. Pray the line, asking the Holy Spirit why it is important to you.

✧ Converse with the Holy Spirit about your life of prayer. What do you pray about? Do you pray in the good times as well as the bad? How much time do you listen to the word of God? Do you open your heart to God about your experiences? Is there any topic you are ashamed to pray about? Do you give thanks and praise in prayer?

You may want to write down your dialog with Jesus about these questions.

✧ Pray these words of Louise several times: "You have every reason to trust in God. . . . God will never fail to let you know how agreeable this manner of acting is to Him." Then tell God exactly how you feel about what is most discouraging, dysfunctional, and fearful in your life right now. You can open up with everything that you cannot tell anyone else. God can take it. Maybe in letting loose with God you can let go yourself.

✧ Try this practice of prayer: As you enter any room where you will be spending some time, intentionally recall the presence of God with words like, "God is present. This is holy ground" or some other phrase.

✧ Louise realized that prayer is essential to sincere service to our suffering brothers and sisters. Spend some time in prayer asking God to enlighten you regarding the meaning of your mission in life. Pray for strength to carry it out.

✧ Pray a litany of thanksgiving for all the gifts God has given you; for instance, "For Sarah's wonderful smile and kindly disposition, I thank you, God," or "For the inspiring faith and peaceful death of my patient, Tom, I thank you, God."

✧ For some moments reflect on these words of Louise: "It is your prayers . . . which attract from the goodness of God all His graces." Then, offer your petitions to God about anything for which you need strength and guidance.

God's Word

So I say to you: Ask, and it will be given to you; search, and you will find; knock, and the door will be opened to you. For everyone who asks receives; everyone who searches finds; everyone who knocks will have the door opened. (Luke 11:9–10)

Closing prayer: Let us pray the prayer of Louise:

I praise God with all my heart for the guidance of His Providence in all things, especially in the duty which His goodness has confided to you. I hope that your gratitude will place you in the disposition necessary to receive the graces you need to serve your sick poor in a spirit of gentleness and great compassion, in imitation of Our Lord who acted this way with the most unfortunate. (*Writings*, p. 434)

✧ Meditation 13 ✧

Celebrating Friendship

Theme: God sends us the priceless gift of friendship. Like any gift, this one needs to be cherished, deepened, and celebrated.

Opening prayer: Holy Friend, help me to be open to your friendship and to be free to extend it to others, especially those most in need. May I cherish, share with, and help my friends, my companions on the journey.

About Louise

For thirty-five years, Vincent and Louise journeyed together, learning to know, esteem, and respect each other. The same mission to serve poor people brought Vincent and Louise together. They spent some years getting to know each other and collaborating intensely. As Louise assumed more independent leadership of the Daughters of Charity, and Vincent's responsibilities expanded, a period of some tensions and difficulty challenged their relationship, but ultimately strengthened it.

Vincent and Louise knew that they could count on each other in all circumstances. Louise went to Vincent, told him what was in her heart. Vincent listened. He would not take away the pain or the worry, he would simply listen. Vincent strengthened her for the journey.

Likewise, Louise was a gift and a grace to Vincent. She listened to him and brought gentleness, tenderness, and peace to his heart. This letter to Vincent provides a glimpse into their relationship:

> Another thing I find most necessary, and of great use, is that your Charity, if you think it appropriate, take the trouble to write a letter to all our sisters, which shows a bit of dissatisfaction with them, and which encourages them. Just as true, my Most Honored Father, is the fact that this poor little Company is truly suffering under my wretched guidance! I also think that God will soon deliver it from this captivity, which is such a great obstacle to the perfection of His work. I myself have great reason to fear dying in my hardheartedness if your Charity does not help me. (*Writings*, p. 194)

To this request, Vincent replied in a seven-page letter. In fact, their extensive correspondence remains the best testament to their relationship.

Vincent was never far from her thoughts, and Louise expressed her love through her concern for his health or in seeking news of him. For instance, in one letter, she encouraged Vincent to express his feelings of grief and loss when a loved confrere died:

> It truly seems that our Lord is the sole proprietor general of the Congregation of the Mission, since He disposes of the good subjects He has given it in this way . . . Am I not truly bold, my Most Honored Father, to dare to mix my tears with your usual submission to the guidance of Divine Providence, my weaknesses with the strength God has given you in order to bear the great share in His sufferings? . . . For love of Him, give nature what it needs for its relief and what you need for your health. (*Writings*, p. 415)

One of the most tender references to Vincent is found in a letter to Father Antoine Portail in which she unabashedly urged him to gather more information about the man both of them loved dearly. "Since you are going to Gascony, oh Monsieur, do not forget to find out all you can, so that you can answer all the questions I am going to ask you in an effort to know better the person [Vincent] who is the dearest in the world to us" (*Writings*, p. 163).

The affection, concern, and esteem was mutual. Vincent's letters constantly manifest his friendship with Louise:

> What shall I tell you about the one whom your heart loves so dearly in Our Lord?

> Mon Dieu, my dear daughter, how your letter and the thoughts you sent me console me! Indeed, I must confess to you that the feeling has spread through every part of my soul, and with all the more pleasure, since they let me see you are in the state God wants of you. (*Vincentian Heritage*, vol. 11, no. 1, p. 67)

The common ground of their relationship was their love for God and poor people. They found God in their own heart, in each other's heart, and in the hearts of the poor.

Pause: Bring to mind your most intimate friends; just hold them in your heart.

Louise's Words

> If your heart has been as steadfast as you tell me, oh, then I love it with all mine and even more because, since it is the love of God which produces such effects in it, it must be honored and cherished. I beg this holy love to fill it completely. . . . Let us truly love each other in Him, but let us love Him in each other since we are His. (*Writings*, pp. 158–159)

Reflection

Human beings need the acceptance, support, and love of true friends if they are to live lives of faith, hope, and charity. Many of the great saints have been friends: Louise and Vincent, Jane de Chantal and Francis de Sales, Teresa of Avila and John of the Cross, Clare and Francis of Assisi, Dorothy Day and Peter

Maurin, to say nothing of Jesus and Mary of Magdala. These friends journeyed together, bonded by the God who is love. In their time and space, these friends brought the Good News to their brothers and sisters not only through their inspired words and charitable deeds, but also by the example of friendship that they gave.

Friendship is one way of loving: it is the heart of the Good News. Love means to seek and then foster the good of others in the context of their concrete situations. The love of friends is characterized by mutual caring between two people, loyalty, acceptance, honesty, availability, generous help, and equality. Friends are capable of helping each other to achieve what is good. Given this description, obviously Louise and Vincent were friends.

Louise and Vincent placed all their resources at the service of Jesus Christ in the person of homeless, orphaned, hungry, sick, and imprisoned people. They helped each other love God and achieve what is good. Individually they may have still done remarkable service; together they revolutionized ministry to God's poor.

The friendship of Louise and Vincent can remind us of the importance of friends in becoming more Christ-like. Indeed, how can we have strength for the journey and carry our crosses and celebrate God's miracles without friends?

✧ A popular T-shirt shows a circle of people, holding hands and dancing. The caption reads, "A family is a circle of friends who love you." Draw a circle of your friends, the people who accept you, who give and receive equally and mutually, who help you achieve what is good, who have loved life into you. Print the initials of a different friend on each figure.

Pray a prayer of gratitude for each friend. To express your gratitude for and joy about your friendship, write them a letter or give them a call. Better yet, visit with them.

✧ Louise found that hard times also produced deep friendships. Out of difficulties emerged great discoveries, recoveries, and lost values. Recall some adversity that you went through with a friend. Ponder the ways in which this mutually shared adversity led to a deeper understanding between you.

✦ Acquaintances are coworkers, schoolmates, neighbors, and social contacts with whom we touch base occasionally. We know who they are and a little about them. We say hello to each other and might make small talk with them. *Collaborators* are people with whom we have a common interest or project for which we need the help of one another. In these relationships, the two people band together because each gives something to the other.

Write down a list of five acquaintances and five collaborators. Which of them might become a friend? How could you nurture your relationship?

Pray for each of these acquaintances and collaborators, remembering that the friendship between Vincent and Louise started in acquaintance and collaboration.

✦ Recall one important friendship that ended. Reflect on the forces at work that caused this friendship to end. Then answer this question: Knowing what I know now, could we have saved our friendship? Pray for this former friend. If you think that the friendship could be renewed, take action to do so.

God's Word

I thank my God whenever I think of you, and every time I pray for you all, I always pray with joy for your partnership in the gospel from the very first day up to the present. I am quite confident that the One who began a good work in you will go on completing it until the Day of Jesus Christ comes. It is only right that I should feel like this towards you all, because you have a place in my heart, since you have all shared together in the grace that has been mine, both my chains and my work defending and establishing the gospel. For God will testify for me how much I long for you all with the warm longing of Christ Jesus; it is my prayer that your love for one another may grow more and more with the knowledge and complete understanding that will help you to come to true discernment, so that you will be innocent and free of any trace of guilt when the Day of Christ comes, entirely filled with the fruits of uprightness through Jesus Christ, for the glory and praise of God. (Philippians 1:3–11)

Closing prayer: Let us pray the prayer of Louise:

May my life be solely for Jesus and my neighbor so that, by means of this unifying love, I may love all that Jesus loves, and through the power of this love which has as its center the eternal love of God for His creatures, I may obtain from His goodness the graces which His mercy wills to bestow upon me. (*Writings*, p. 786)

Love One Another

Theme: If the Daughters of Charity were to remain steadfast in their service to poor people, they needed the mutual support of a community. Louise understood that anyone trying to lead a Christian life needed the help of a community: "This is necessary in order to live as Christians" (*Writings*, p. 230). So she instructed the sisters on how to create communities that would model the virtues found in the early Christian communities.

Opening prayer: God of love, teach me to appreciate and create community as much as I am able, wherever I am.

About Louise

The Company of the Daughters of Charity had been founded to serve poor people. Service nourished the sisters' prayer and gave meaning to life in community. In turn, community life revitalized the sisters' service. So, using the Trinity as her example, Louise consistently reminded the sisters to live in harmony: "I prayed also that He might be the strong and loving bond that unites the hearts of all the sisters in imitation of the union of the three Divine Persons" (*Writings*, p. 122).

Louise helped the communities of each type of ministry establish basic, agreed-upon guidelines for life together. All the communities were to pray, work, and recreate together, and share the talents of all members. To Sister Laurence at Bernay, Louise wrote:

> I have the impression that the two of you are living together in great peace and with the desire of animating one another to strive for union and cordiality. This creates a climate in which you communicate with one another, telling one another what you did while you were apart and letting one another know where you are going when you leave the house. In this instance one of you acts from an obligation of submission while the other has the duty of support and courtesy. The same applies to your community exercises. If one of you is sad, let her overcome herself so as to recreate with her sister. At the same time, let the one who is cheerful moderate her exuberance so as to accommodate herself to the mood of her sister and, little by little, draw her out of her melancholy. All this should be done for the love of God and to avoid listening to the temptation that might cause you to want to go elsewhere to unburden your soul and to seek satisfaction. (*Writings*, p. 463)

Communication, sensitivity, cheerfulness, flexibility, and perseverance were foundational for community building among the Daughters.

However, Louise was realistic enough to know that living community life could be exacting and that human foibles would often cause disharmony. So when the sisters needed confronting, Louise could be direct and firm. To Sister Madeleine at Angers, she wrote:

> I am apprehensive about suspicions and rash judgments. They often cause little troubles. In the name of God, my dear Sister, I beg you to show support and cordiality among you and to practice cheerfulness. (*Writings*, p. 200)

In another letter to Sister Madeleine, Louise scolded her:

> My God, my poor sister, I cannot hide the pain I felt. . . . I thought you were above these small weaknesses. Do we think, my dear Sister, that we should never be contradicted?

Do we think that everyone must give in to our wishes, and that they are obliged to find everything we do and say good? Do we think we can do as we wish without being held accountable? (*Writings*, p. 129)

Louise could confront her sisters, but she praised them too. Pointing out the relationship between community and their ministry, Louise praised one community of sisters this way:

I found particular consolation in your way of life which is permeated with cordiality and mutual support. I was greatly comforted also by the respect, modesty, and charity with which you act. It is in this way, my dear Sisters, that you must edify the public and not be persons who only bear the name and wear the habit of the Daughters of Charity. (*Writings*, pp. 642–643)

Pause: What sort of community do you have or want?

Louise's Words

The Rule of the Daughters of Charity states:

They shall cherish one another as Sisters who profess to honor the spirit of Our Lord by the practice of charity which is the virtue He practiced most perfectly on earth and which He most strongly recommended to His followers. To this end they shall visit one another and assist one another in sickness and in health. They shall pray for one another especially in case of sickness or death. . . . In short, they should do all in their power to help one another to leave this world in a good state. (*Writings*, pp. 709–710)

Reflection

Louise envisioned the sisters warming themselves at the fire of mutual love within the community before going out to share this fire with the poor people living in a harsh and dreadful world. Christ and the early Christians were the inspiration for community life.

The need for community exists in all of us and in every culture. Christians are united by belief in the Triune God revealed in the life, death, and Resurrection of Jesus Christ. Belief in Christ expresses itself in charity, common prayer, and mutual sharing. Indeed, the early Christians were known by their love for one another. As Louise said, community "is necessary in order to live as Christians."

Louise urged the sisters to create community not just for themselves, but because they would be more effective in their charity. United together they could accomplish more than their individual efforts. In addition, a caring community showed the poor that harmony, peace, and love were possible among people inspired by Christ.

✦ Most of us belong to a variety of communities; that is, groups of people sharing some common values and interests and caring for one another. Identify the various communities to which you belong. What do you do to actively build these communities?

✦ If there is a group of people with whom you would like to develop a sense of community, what beliefs, values, and interests could draw you together? What actions could you take to invite these people to form a community?

✦ Thank God for the communities that you are a part of. Name people with whom you are particularly grateful to share community. Ask God's gift of wisdom and charity for people who do not seem to fit into the community but try to belong.

✦ Is there some organization or activity of your parish, family, or local community to which you could contribute your time, talents, and energy? Consider how you could take part to better the community.

✦ Pray over this statement of Louise: "They should do all in their power to help one another to leave this world in a good state." Ask the Holy Spirit to help you understand what this means for you and what you can do for the common good.

God's Word

Be united in imitating me [Paul]. Keep your eyes fixed on those who act according to the example you have from me. . . .

So then, my . . . dear friends whom I miss so much, my joy and my crown, hold firm in the Lord, dear friends. . . .

Always be joyful, then, in the Lord; I repeat, be joyful. Let your good sense be obvious to everybody. The Lord is near. Never worry about anything; but tell God all your desires of every kind in prayer and petition shot through with gratitude, and the peace of God which is beyond our understanding will guard your hearts and your thoughts in Christ Jesus. . . . Let your minds be filled with everything that is true, everything that is honorable, everything that is upright and pure, everything that we love and admire—with whatever is good and praiseworthy. Keep doing everything you learnt from me and were told by me and have heard or seen me doing. Then the God of peace will be with you. (Philippians 3:17; 4:1–9)

Closing prayer: Complete your meditation by praying Psalm 133:

How good it is, how pleasant,
for God's people to live in unity.
It is like the precious oil
running down from Aaron's head and beard,
down to the collar of his robes.
It is like the dew on Mount Hermon
falling on the hills of Zion.
For there Yahweh has promised a blessing,
life that never ends.

Humility

Theme: The Spirit of God forms us when we have humility. This virtue implies that we fully acknowledge our total dependence on God's freely given, undeserved grace. The humble heart seeks God's guidance, follows God's will, and treats all brothers and sisters with profound respect.

Opening prayer: Gracious God, teach me humility. Teach me to be humble of heart so that I may be ready to respond to the absolute love that you have for me and for all your people.

About Louise

The humility of a caring God who would become incarnate so that we could live in relationship with others fascinated and inspired Louise. From Jesus, she learned the humility of being human. In her retreat notes she remarks, "He came as humbly as can be imagined so that we might be more free to approach Him" (*Writings*, p. 700).

One result of embracing her common humanity was that Louise valued the advice of other people and sought it. On the evening of 30 December 1656, after Vincent had reminded her to place steadfast reliance on God, she wrote:

> This remark made me understand that I had been hasty in my zeal and that my own passions had sometimes come

into play. It also taught me that I should serve souls in their needs by another practice, that of turning to God by an interior act of confidence and trusting Him to accomplish by His grace and goodness all that I could not do. (*Writings*, p. 815)

Part of humility is listening to the wisdom of other people and to God's word.

Another aspect of humility is relying on God's providence even as we do our best to deal with the challenges of life. To a troubled Sister Jeanne Lepintre who, among other complaints, could not confide in her spiritual director, Louise advised:

> How fortunate you are, my dear Sister, to know yourself so well and to be so deeply devoted to the most holy will of God which is our sole good if it is accomplished in us. With all my heart, I pray that it will be revealed to your heart and teach you how to bear with yourself. . . .
>
> Recall, my dear Sister, the great Saint Teresa who was much busier than we and charged with affairs of much greater importance and who often needed advice. Although the advisors she wanted were absent, she was so simple and humble that she freely sought advice from those whom Providence sent her as directors. She listened to them as if God were speaking to her. She was satisfied with the essential and calmly abandoned the rest to the guidance of God. I am sure that you know from experience, my dear Sister, that when human beings fail us, God reveals Himself more abundantly to us. (*Writings*, p. 427)

In the context of a common humanity, redeemed by a compassionate, humble Christ, Louise developed a profound respect for all persons: the Daughters, the Ladies of Charity, and the poor people among whom she worked. She constantly reiterated the need for humility when serving sick or needy people. Sister Claude Brigide had outlined her difficulties in a letter to Louise. Louise responded:

> Trust that [the difficulties] will pass. . . . May they keep you humble so that you may love and esteem our good sisters and show them, in matters concerning the service of the poor, the submission you owe them because of their

long experience in the house. . . . Please God by serving your masters [the poor] and His dear members with devotion, gentleness and humility. Do not be upset if your senses rebel, but reflect that our good God is satisfied by a heart filled with good will. I beg His goodness to fill yours with His holy love in which I remain, my dear Sister, your sister and servant. (*Writings*, p. 81)

Pause: Do you think of trials as reminders of your own needy humanity?

Louise's Words

I must practice great humility; . . . abandon myself continuously to the Providence of God; imitate, insofar as I am able, the life of Our Lord who came on earth to accomplish the holy will of God His Father; assist my neighbor to the best of my ability both corporally and spiritually for the love which God has for all of us equally. (*Writings*, p. 784)

Blessed be God for everything! May He grant the Company the strength and generosity to maintain within itself the primitive spirit that Jesus instilled in it through His Spirit and by His holy maxims. Let us often give ourselves to God so as to obtain from His goodness the generosity needed to advance His glory by fulfilling His designs on the Company. (*Writings*, p. 673)

Reflection

Louise's emphasis on humility was connected to her imitation of Christ. Her actions, attitudes, and instructions always depended on her contemplation of Jesus as humble of heart.

To be humble implies that we know the truth about our earthly limitations and also about our divine giftedness. Humility keeps us planted on the ground (in Latin, *humus*), conscious of our real condition: complete dependence on the will of God who nourishes and loves us.

Humility also reminds us that all people are our equals before the God who created us. All human beings deserve our respect, honor, charity, and service. The humble Jesus came to save all of humankind, not just the rich, famous, righteous, or good. He urged us to unite with him in building the Reign of God among our sisters and brothers. The virtue of humility frees us from pride, self-righteousness, and arrogance that separates us from other people. In this way, we can become one people of God (see John 17:22).

✧ Reread the "Louise's Words" section. Ask the Holy Spirit to make clear the implications of her words for you. Then compose your own mission statement, a summary of how you want to cooperate with God's will in your circumstances.

✧ What experiences in your life have reminded you of your common humanity with other fallible, needy, vulnerable people? Do an inventory of these grounding experiences. Then reflect on how you responded in each instance and whether you grew in humility and charity as a result.

Compose a litany of thanksgiving for all the reminders in your life that tell you that you are not God but a fallible, needful human being who is gifted by a loving God: for example, "For the shame I feel when my sharp tongue hurts those I love, thank you, God."

Then pray a litany of thanks for the gifts, skills, talents, and personality that God has given you; for instance, "For being able to sing joyfully, thank you, God."

You might write down your litanies so they can be reminders for you.

✧ Recall the holy presence of God. Pray slowly and repeatedly, "Jesus, humble of heart, make my heart like yours."

✧ Is there a situation in your life right now that you find humbling? Ask yourself how this situation can be God's call to continuing conversion. What attitude could you bring to this situation so that it could become freeing and empowering for you?

✧ Begin a habit of visiting and helping a shut-in person; a lonely relative or neighbor; a friend living with terminal cancer, AIDS, or other disease; or someone else who needs assistance.

God's Word

You should all agree among yourselves and be sympathetic; love [each other], have compassion and be self-effacing. . . .

Humility towards one another must be the garment you all wear constantly, because God opposes the proud. . . . The God of all grace who called you to eternal glory in Christ will restore you, . . . confirm, strengthen and support you. (1 Peter 3:8; 5:5–10)

Closing prayer: Let us pray the prayer of Louise:

I praise God with all my heart for the good desires which, in His goodness, He continues to stir up. . . . Teach [our heart] humility by saying to it "Let us accomplish well what we are permitted to do . . . and let us rest assured that Our Lord will be pleased with us." (*Writings*, p. 481)

C·H·A·R·I·T·Y

✦ For Further Reading ✦

Calvet, Jean. *Louise de Marillac: A Portrait.* New York: G. F. Pullen, 1959.

Dirvin, Joseph. *Louise de Marillac.* New York: Farrar, Straus & Giroux, 1970.

Flinton, Margaret. *Louise de Marillac: Social Aspect of Her Work.* New York: New City Press, 1992.

Gobillon, Nicolas. *The Life of Mademoiselle Le Gras.* London: The Ridgeway, 1984.

Sullivan, Louise, ed. and trans. *Spiritual Writings of Louise de Marillac: Correspondence and Thoughts.* New York: New City Press, 1991.

Vincentian Heritage. vol. 11, no.1 and vol. 12, no. 2. Vincentian Studies Institute. Cape Girardeau, Missouri: Concord Publishing House, 1990, 1991.

Acknowledgments *(continued)*

The excerpts on pages 13–14, 23, 26–27, and 67 are from *Louise de Marillac,* by Joseph I. Dirvin (New York: Farrar, Straus and Giroux, 1970), pages ix, 142, 319, and 387, respectively. Copyright © 1970 by Farrar, Straus and Giroux. All rights reserved.

All of the quotes from *Spiritual Writings of Louise de Marillac: Correspondence and Thoughts,* edited and translated by Louise Sullivan (New York: New City Press, 1991) are used by permission of the Daughters of Charity of Saint Vincent de Paul.

The quotes from *Vincentian Heritage,* vol. 11, no. 1 (1990) and vol. 12, no. 2 (1991) are used with permission of the Vincentian Studies Institute.

The two excerpts on page 25 and the excerpt on page 26 are from *Louise de Marillac: Social Aspect of Her Work,* by Margaret Flinton (New York: New City Press, 1992), pages 112, 96, and 98, respectively. Copyright © 1992 by Margaret Flinton.

Titles in the Companions for the Journey Series

Praying with Catherine McAuley   Forthcoming

Praying with Catherine of Siena

Praying with Clare of Assisi

Praying with Dominic

Praying with Dorothy Day

Praying with Elizabeth Seton

Praying with Francis of Assisi

Praying with Hildegard of Bingen

Praying with Ignatius of Loyola

Praying with John Baptist de La Salle

Praying with John of the Cross

Praying with Julian of Norwich

Praying with Louise de Marillac

Praying with Teresa of Ávila

Praying with Thérèse of Lisieux

Praying with Thomas Merton

Praying with Vincent de Paul

Order from your local religious bookstore or from

Saint Mary's Press
702 TERRACE HEIGHTS
WINONA MN 55987-1320
USA
1-800-533-8095